Project
Management

Dr. Prasun Bhattacharjee

DEDICATION

To my dearest family, friends, and all those who have supported me on this incredible journey—this book is dedicated to you. Your unwavering belief in me, your encouragement, and your love has fueled my passion and propelled me forward. Each word on these pages is a reflection of our shared experiences, our laughter, our tears, and our triumphs. You have been my pillars of strength, my guiding light, and my greatest inspiration. This book is a testament to our collective spirit and the power of human connection.

Thank you for being a part of my story.

CONTENTS

ACKNOWLEDGMENTS

I am deeply grateful to the following individuals who have enriched my life and supported me throughout the creation of this book:

To my teachers, who ignited the spark of knowledge within me and guided me along the path of learning. Your wisdom, patience, and dedication have been instrumental in shaping my understanding of the subject matter. I am indebted to you for imparting not only knowledge but also a love for exploration and intellectual growth.

To my students, who have been a constant source of inspiration. Your curiosity, enthusiasm, and insightful questions have challenged me to delve deeper into the subject matter and strive for clarity in my explanations. It is through your engagement and active participation that I have grown as an educator and author.

I would also like to express my gratitude to my colleagues and mentors for their invaluable support and encouragement throughout this writing process. Your feedback, guidance, and willingness to share your expertise have been instrumental in shaping the content of this book.

Furthermore, I extend my heartfelt appreciation to my friends and family for their unwavering belief in me and their constant encouragement. Your love, understanding, and patience have provided the emotional support I needed to pursue this endeavor.

Finally, I want to thank the readers of this book for their interest and trust. It is my sincerest hope that the knowledge and insights presented here will be of value to you in your journeys of discovery.

Without the support and contributions of these incredible individuals, this book would not have been possible. Thank you all for being a part of this meaningful endeavor.

1 FUNDAMENTALS OF PROJECT MANAGEMENT

Project management is the procedure of preparing, forming, and controlling the accomplishment of a project. It comprises a variety of actions, from explaining project objectives and purposes to handling resources, time, and funds. Project management is indispensable for confirming that projects are finished on time, within budgetary limits, and to the preferred quality level.

1.1 How can we define a Project?

A project is an exclusive, impermanent attempt with a well-defined commencement and culmination that is assumed to attain an explicit aim. It is a single-time action, nothing like continuing processes that are envisioned to yield recurring outcomes. A project possibly will include the conception of a novel product, service, or procedure, the execution of an innovative system or technology, or the dispensing of a definite result, for instance, an incident or building development.

1.2 Characteristics of a Project

Projects are characteristically categorized by the subsequent fundamentals:

1.2.1 Definite Purposes

Projects are premeditated to realize precise aims. These purposes must be undoubtedly demarcated at the beginning of the project.

1.2.2 Restricted Timeframe

Projects have distinct commencement and termination date. They are impermanent and have an explicit timeframe for the conclusion.

1.2.3 Exclusive Deliverables

Projects render exclusive products, services, or consequences that are dissimilar from those formed by continuing activities.

1.2.4 Definite Resources

Projects necessitate definite resources, containing individuals, apparatus, and materials. These resources might be unlike those expended in continuing procedures.

1.2.5 Cross-functional Teams

Projects frequently comprise individuals from diverse operative fields and divisions. Project teams are characteristically cross-functional and are formed by people with dissimilar proficiencies and knowledge.

1.2.6 Risk Management

Projects include jeopardies, as well as technical, ecological, fiscal, and other risks. Project managers ought to recognize and cope with these jeopardies during the entire project lifespan.

1.2.7 Gradual Enhancement

Projects are regularly subject to modification, and as additional information becomes accessible, project strategies might require to be reworked or reorganized. This procedure is termed gradual expansion.

PROJECT MANAGEMENT

On the whole, a project is an impermanent venture commenced to realize a precise objective or purpose. It includes a clear series of jobs, resources, and timelines and entails cautious preparation, supervision, and implementation to confirm triumph.

1.3 Essential Norms

1.3.1 Identifying Aims and Purposes

The primary phase in project management is to outline the project's aims and intentions. This encompasses defining what the project goals are to realize, what means will be required, and what timelines ought to be pursued.

1.3.2 Creating a Project Plan

After the project targets and purposes have been demarcated, a project plan ought to be settled. This plan must comprise an exhaustive itemization of responsibilities, timelines, and resources essential for every phase of the project.

1.3.3 Allocating Tasks and Assignments

All associates of the project team must be allotted definite responsibilities and assignments. This guarantees that everybody recognizes what is demanded of them and facilitates to avert misperception or repetition of endeavor.

1.3.4 Handling Resources

Efficient resource management is essential to envisage accomplishment. This includes scrutinizing the accessibility of resources (for instance people, apparatus, and materials), assigning resources as required, and guaranteeing that resources are expended competently.

1.3.5 Observing Development

Consistent growth supervising is indispensable to guarantee that the project is heading in the right direction. This comprises following the conclusion of tasks, recognizing probable disputes, and adopting counteractive action as required.

1.3.6 Handling Risks

Each project includes risks, and project managers ought to recognize possible risks and develop tactics to alleviate them. This contains evaluating possible risks, categorizing suitable retorts, and applying risk management policies.

1.3.7 Conveying Effectually

Efficient communication is important to confirm that everybody participating in the project is conscious of the project status, objectives, and timelines. This encompasses steady communiqué with team associates, stakeholders, and customers.

1.3.8 Assessing and Progressing

As soon as the project is finished, it's imperative to assess the consequences and recognize fields for enhancement. This includes reconsidering project conclusions, investigating project execution, and expanding the understanding gained to advance forthcoming projects.

Generally, project management necessitates cautious preparation, valuable communiqué, and expert guidance. By following these central philosophies, project managers can guarantee that their projects are accomplished fruitfully, on time, and within budget.

1.4 Significance in Daily Life

Project management is a crucial competence that can be harnessed to several facets of our day-to-day lives. Whether we're arranging a holiday, renovating a building, or arranging a charity occasion, project management supports us accomplish our aims competently and effectually. The next are particular motives because which project management is indispensable in our day-to-day lives:

1.4.1 Time Management

Time management is a vital characteristic of project management. By generating a schedule and timeline for our projects, we can guarantee that we conclude them punctually and evade eleventh-hour haste. It benefits us to rank responsibilities and confirm that we are expending our time effectually.

1.4.2 Cost Controlling

Project management can support us to administer our supplies successfully. By preparing beforehand and making a budget, we can preclude extravagance and confirm that we are remaining within our means.

1.4.3 Managing Risk

Project management permits us to antedate probable menaces and cultivate exigency tactics to alleviate them. It aids us to recognize possible hitches and create policies to minimalize their effect.

1.4.4 Message

Communication is crucial to the feat of any project. Project management reassures communiqué between team associates, stakeholders, and merchants, guaranteeing that one and all are on the similar page and functioning in the direction of a shared ambition.

1.4.5 Objective Establishing

Project management supports us to establish well-defined aims and purposes. Through outlining our purposes, we can grow a roadmap for realizing them, and assess our development along the way.

In conclusion, project management is an indispensable ability that can be employed in numerous characteristics of our everyday lives. It assists us to manage our time and resources efficiently, forestall possible risks, connect successfully, and accomplish our ambitions competently. By utilizing project management ideologies in our regular lives, we can become more prepared, creative, and effective.

1.5 Example of Implementation

Project management is a crucial field that aids establishments organize, performing, and delivering projects efficaciously. In today's high-speed and dynamic commercial atmosphere, project management has turned out to be more significant than ever before. In this article, we will look at a contemporary case of project management and how it is being utilized to attain professional aims.

Instance: Implementing a Brand-new E-commerce Application

Assume that a big merchandising business needs to employ an original e-commerce application to enhance its virtual trades and consumer experience. The project will engage several teams and sponsors, incorporating IT, advertising, sales, and customer assistance. The firm has put a stringent time limit of eight months to introduce the new-fangled application, and the cost for the project is $8 million.

To handle this venture, the corporation will require an all-inclusive project management strategy that comprises the succeeding components:

1.5.1 Project Prospect

The primary phase in project management is to outline the project prospect, which contains the purposes, deliverables, timelines, and finances. In this situation, the project opportunity would be to put into operation a novel e-commerce application that meets the corporation's commercial goals and is launched within eight months and $8 million.

1.5.2 Project Team

The following phase is to accumulate a project team that comprises the suited individuals with the essential proficiencies and knowledge to deliver the project. In this circumstance, the project team would involve IT experts, vendors, salespeople, client facility delegates, and project executives.

1.5.3 Project Strategy

The project strategy is a comprehensive roadmap that defines the responsibilities, timelines and means required to finish the project. In this situation, the project design would comprise responsibilities such as choosing the e-commerce application, designing the client interface, combining with prevailing procedures, checking, and educating.

1.5.4 Project Finances

The project budget summarizes the expenses connected with the project, involving workforce, resources, and other expenditures. In this circumstance, the project budget would be $8 million.

1.5.5 Project Risks

Project stakes are the possible happenings that might affect the venture's accomplishment, and they must be recognized and coped with proactively. In this situation, some of the jeopardies can contain technological problems, postponements in merchant supply, and variations in client necessities.

1.5.6 Project Communiqué

Effectual communication is crucial to project management, and the project team must have a clear-cut communication idea that summarizes how the information will be communicated among participants. In this case, the project team would utilize frequent status consultations, email updates, and project management software to interconnect.

1.5.7 Project Implementation

The implementation stage is when the project strategy is enforced, and the project team acts to deliver the project goals. In this circumstance, the project team would act on responsibilities for example choosing the e-commerce application, designing the operator interface, and amalgamating with prevailing arrangements.

1.5.8 Project Supervising and Handling

Throughout the project implementation time, the project team should check development in contrast to the project strategy, recognize any problems, and take remedial action if essential. In this situation, the project administrator would employ project management software to follow the evolution and find any issues.

1.5.9 Project Conclusion

As soon as the project is finished, the project team must perform a post-mortem assessment to assess the plan's accomplishment and recognize the experiences gathered. In this circumstance, the project team would appraise the accomplishment of the newfangled e-commerce application and find any spheres for enhancement.

1.5.10 Inference

Instigating a new e-commerce application is merely one instance of how project management is employed in today's commercial ecosystem. Project management is a decisive field that aids establishments attain their purposes, whether it is introducing fresh merchandise, developing a new facility, or applying a new arrangement. By ensuring the finest systems and utilizing project management software, project executives can propose, perform, and deliver fruitful ventures that meet the requirements of participants and deliver actual professional worth.

1.6 Exercise

1. What is project management and why is it important?
2. What are the key differences between a project and ongoing operations?
3. What are the primary responsibilities of a project manager?
4. What are the five stages of the project life cycle?
5. What is a project charter and what is its purpose?
6. What is a work breakdown structure (WBS) and why is it used in project management?
7. What are the main components of a project management plan?
8. What is the critical path in project management and how is it determined?
9. How do you identify and manage project risks?
10. What is the role of a project sponsor and why is sponsorship important?
11. What is the triple constraint in project management and how does it affect project planning?
12. How do you create and manage a project budget?
13. What is a stakeholder and how do you identify and engage stakeholders in a project?

14. What is the purpose of a project kickoff meeting and what should be included in it?

15. How do you define and measure project success?

16. What is the role of a project team and how do you build an effective team?

17. How do you manage project communications and ensure effective stakeholder engagement?

18. What is change management in the context of project management and why is it important?

19. How do you handle project scope changes and scope creep?

20. What is the difference between a project manager and a project leader?

21. What are some common project management methodologies (e.g., waterfall, Agile, Scrum) and when are they appropriate to use?

22. How do you conduct a project post-mortem or lessons-learned session?

23. What is the difference between project risk and issue management?

24. How do you manage project dependencies and constraints?

25. What are the main components of a project communication plan?

26. How do you establish and track project milestones?

27. What is a project baseline and why is it important?

28. How do you conduct effective project meetings?

29. What is the role of a project management office (PMO) and what services does it provide?

30. How do you manage project quality and ensure deliverables meet the required standards?

2 History and Future

Project management has been in the environs for thousands of years, even though it has progressed drastically over time. The idea of handling a project, or an impermanent effort to form an exclusive product or service, can be trailed back to the building of the Great Pyramid of Giza in Egypt approximately 2560 BC. Nevertheless, project management as a solemn vocation and field did not appear until the 20th century. In this article, we will delve into the past of project management, its development, and crucial achievements that have steered the contemporary system of project management.

2.1 Initial Instances

As cited, one of the primitive instances of project management can be perceived in the creation of the Great Pyramid of Giza. This colossal venture comprised synchronizing the endeavors of tens of thousands of laborers, engineers, designers, and other experts to construct one of the utmost perceptible constructions on the planet. It necessitated cautious preparation, resource administration, and risk organization, all of which are indispensable characteristics of present-day project management.

Another primary instance of project management can be realized in the creation of the Roman aqueducts in the first century AD. These remarkable constructions were planned to supply water from far-off sources to metropolises and settlements throughout the Roman Empire. The creation of these aqueducts needed watchful preparation, harmonization, and resource supervision to confirm that the water streamed competently and consistently.

Project management has an extensive past in India, with countless instances of projects dating back to primeval times. In primordial India, project management was employed to construct intricate buildings, for instance, places of worship, castles, and irrigation systems. One of the initial cases of project management in primeval India is the creation of the Indus Valley Civilization, which was constructed between 2600 BCE and 1900 BCE. The Indus Valley Civilization was one of the world's largest and most progressive civilizations, and its towns were recognized for their state-of-the-art urban development, highly developed drainage systems, and extensive construction projects.

One more specimen of project management in olden India is the building of the Taj Mahal, which was constructed between 1632 and 1653 by Mughal Ruler Shah Jahan in reminiscence of his wife Mumtaz Mahal. The creation of the Taj Mahal required a band of planners, engineers, and craftspeople who functioned collectively to plan and create the building. The project engaged cautious preparation and implementation, with the usage of forward-thinking construction practices, such as the use of white marble and intricate stone carvings.

Other examples of project management in ancient India include the construction of the Konark Sun Temple, the Kumbhalgarh Fort, and the ancient irrigation systems of the Indus Valley and the Maurya Empire.

These ancient projects demonstrate the importance of project management in achieving complex objectives, even in the absence of modern technology and tools. They also illustrate the need for careful planning, execution, and collaboration among team members to achieve successful project outcomes. Today, project management continues to play a crucial role in India's development, with a growing number of large-scale projects, such as infrastructure development and smart cities, being undertaken across the country.

2.2 Progression

Although project management has been applied for thousands of years, it was not until the 20th century that it commenced to grow into a formal occupation and field. One of the initial instances of contemporary project management can be perceived in the formation of the Gantt chart by Henry Gantt in the initial years of the 1900s. Gantt was a mechanical engineer who worked on several construction ventures, and he formed the Gantt chart as an instrument to aid him accomplish his projects more effectually.

The Gantt chart is a graphic depiction of a project timetable that indicates the beginning and termination dates of every job and the dependencies between assignments. It is even now extensively applied currently in project management software and is an analytical instrument for project administrators to design and follow their projects.

In the 1950s and 1960s, project management started to acquire more awareness since leading construction projects and government enterprises became more regular. One of the crucial stimulators of this was the construction of the regional highway system in the United States, which necessitated cautious preparation and synchronization throughout several states and organizations.

Throughout this period, project management was instigated to progress into a formal vocation, and numerous establishments were founded to endorse the finest procedures and norms for project supervision. The Project

Management Institute (PMI) was instituted in 1969 and has subsequently become the world's foremost expert organization for project managers. PMI issues the Project Management Body of Knowledge (PMBOK), which is an extensively acknowledged benchmark for project management procedures.

The 1970s and 1980s realized more developments in project management as computers and software turned out to be more extensively accessible. The development of project management software, for instance, Primavera and Microsoft Project, caused it simpler for project managers to design and follow the status of their projects.

In the 1990s and 2000s, project management persisted to advance as businesses started to implement project management policies for instance Agile and Scrum. These approaches are focused on completing projects in quicker repetitions and include added alliance between team associates and stakeholders.

2.3 Future Scope

Project management is expected to progress while establishments implement novel tools and work routines. One of the utmost noteworthy tendencies in project management is the growing utilization of Artificial Intelligence (AI) and Machine Learning (ML) to mechanize repetitive jobs and deliver perceptions about project routine. One more tendency is the rising significance of soft skills for project managers, for instance, communication, guidance, and emotive astuteness.

2.4 Role of AI and ML

AI and ML are transforming the subject of project management by affording potent instruments for handling convoluted projects. This expertise permit project managers to investigate massive expanses of data, make primed judgments, and industrialize repetitive errands, letting them focus on more tactical actions.

AI and ML may benefit project managers to:

Envisage project risks: Through scrutinizing past data and recognizing patterns, AI and ML can envisage project risks and aid project managers to take preemptive actions to mollify them.

Enhance resource apportionment: AI and ML can support project managers to improve resource sharing by examining resource consumption patterns, recognizing blockages, and endorsing resource distribution approaches.

Automate tedious responsibilities: AI and ML can automate monotonous errands, for instance, scheduling, job apportionment, and progress tracking, freeing up project executives to concentrate on more tactical actions.

Enrich decision-making: Through evaluating project data and presenting acumens, AI and ML may benefit project administrators to make informed choices about project prospects, timetables, and funds.

Augment teamwork: AI and ML can increase alliance among project team associates by delivering instantaneous facts and perceptions, aiding communiqué, and cultivating team coordination.

In brief, AI and ML are significant means for project supervisors, empowering them to administer multifaceted projects more competently and effectually. Through leveraging these tools, project administrators can make improved choices, assign supplies more efficiently, and expand association among team affiliates, eventually leading to fruitful project consequences.

2.5 Exercise

1. When did project management as a formal discipline begin to emerge?

2. What were the key historical events that influenced the development of project management?

3. How has project management evolved over the years?

4. Who are some of the pioneers or key figures in the history of project management?

5. What were some early project management methodologies or approaches?

6. How did the growth of technology impact the evolution of project management?

7. What role did the military play in the development of project management?

8. Can you provide examples of notable projects throughout history and how they influenced project management practices?

9. How did the industrial revolution impact project management practices?

10. How did the construction industry contribute to the growth of project management?

11. What were some of the major milestones in the development of project management as a recognized profession?

12. How did the rise of globalization and international collaboration impact project management?

13. What are some key differences between traditional project management and agile project management?

14. How did the development of software and information technology influence project management practices?

15. What were some of the challenges faced by early project managers?

16. How did the growth of project management associations and certifications contribute to the professionalization of the field?

17. How has project management been applied in different industries throughout history?

18. Can you discuss the impact of project management on large-scale infrastructure projects?

19. How did project management methodologies like Six Sigma and Lean contribute to the growth of the field?

20. What are some current trends and challenges in the field of project management?

3 Role of Soft Skills

Project management is not only about managing schedules, investments, and resources. It is also about dealing with people, and this requires a compendium of soft skills that are decisive for achievement. Soft skills are non-technical capabilities that empower people to function effectually with others and attain their goals. In this chapter, we will discover the value of soft skills in project management and why they are imperative for project attainment.

3.1 Communication

Successful communication is one of the utmost vital soft skills for project administrators. Project executives require to connect with team associates, investors, and administrators to keep everybody apprised about the project's advancement, recognize problems, and settle discords. Project executives should be competent to commune efficiently both orally and in writing, utilizing a collection of communication tools, for instance, email, phone, video conferencing, and project management software. They should also be skilled to orient their interaction approach to diverse audiences and circumstances, applying active listening and considerate communiqué to shape confidence and teamwork.

3.2 Leadership

Leadership is another vital soft skill for project supervisors. Project executives need to encourage and persuade their team associates, offer direction, and build a constructive work atmosphere. They should be capable to guide through example, establishing well-defined prospects, and delivering productive advice. They must also be competent to allot responsibilities successfully, energize their team affiliates, and distinguish their supports. Accomplished mentors are also gifted to foresee and cope with opposition, make hard choices, and bear accountability for their activities.

3.3 Problem-Solving

Project administrators must be capable to recognize and resolve complications that occur throughout the project lifespan. They should be talented to congregate information, examine data, and make abreast choices. They must also be bright to reflect analytically and innovatively, utilizing their problem-solving abilities to classify source causes, obtain resolutions, and appraise their efficiency. High-quality problem solvers are also intelligent to forestall probable glitches and take preemptive actions to abate them.

3.4 Time Management

Time management is a vital soft skill for project executives. Project directors need to handle numerous responsibilities and primacies, assign supplies effectually, and guarantee that the project is finalized punctually. They should be competent to prioritize routine tasks, fix pragmatic deadlines, and supervise growth in contrast to targets. They must also be intelligent to acclimatize to variations in the project design, for instance, interruptions or budget limitations, and amend the timetable consequently. Expert time managers are also capable to assign responsibilities effectually, manage their time, and evade deferment.

3.5 Teamwork

Project administrators must be competent to function effectively with others to achieve project objectives. They should be talented to construct and uphold constructive associations with team affiliates, sponsors, and administrators. They must also be capable to cooperate, communicating information, and making resolutions collectively. Excellent team players are also gifted to appreciate and value the diversity of their team associates, listen enthusiastically, and offer encouragement and opinion.

3.6 Emotional Intelligence

Emotional intellect is one more substantial soft skill for project executives. Emotional acumen is the capacity to identify, comprehend, and handle emotions in oneself and others. Project supervisors must be gifted to control their feelings, remain tranquil under stress, and react fittingly to the sentiments of others. They must also be capable to commiserate with others, creating bonds, and developing confidence. Reliable emotional aptitude empowers project executives to foster robust associations, handle disputes effectually, and generate an optimistic work atmosphere.

3.7 Flexibility

In conclusion, project executives need to be adaptable and flexible. Projects are multifaceted and dynamic, and they frequently necessitate modifications to the project strategy. Project executives should be able to become accustomed to variations in the project opportunity, timetable, or financial plan, and alter the scheme consequently. They should also be competent to pick up newfangled proficiencies and skills and keep pace with the up-to-date industry tendencies. Accomplished adaptableness empowers project executives to be preemptive, inventive, and receptive to the requirements of the project.

3.8 Exercise

1. How do soft skills contribute to the success of project management?

2. What are some key soft skills that project managers should possess?

3. How does effective communication impact project management?

4. How do negotiation and conflict resolution skills influence project outcomes?

5. What role does empathy play in project management?

6. How do leadership and influence skills impact project team dynamics?

7. What is the significance of time management and organizational skills in project management?

8. How do adaptability and flexibility contribute to successful project delivery?

9. What role does active listening play in project management?

10. How do problem-solving and critical thinking skills affect project decision-making?

11. How do presentation and persuasion skills help project managers in stakeholder engagement?

12. What impact does emotional intelligence have on project management?

13. How do teamwork and collaboration skills enhance project outcomes?

14. What role do resilience and stress management play in project management?

15. How do cultural sensitivity and diversity awareness impact global project management?

16. How do coaching and mentoring skills support project team development?

17. What is the importance of relationship building and networking in project management?

18. How do creativity and innovation influence project success?

19. What role do risk management and mitigation skills play in project management?

20. How do soft skills contribute to effective project communication and stakeholder engagement?

4 Different Stages of Project Management

Project management is a well-organized method of planning, implementing, and monitoring projects to attain precise targets and purposes. It includes a sequence of separate stages, each with its series of events, deliverables, and challenges. In this chapter, we will discover the diverse stages of project management comprehensively, emphasizing their significant characteristics, influential procedures, and the significance of every segment in confirming project realization.

4.1 Initiation Stage

The initiation stage is the initial situation of any project. Its key purpose is to outline the venture's intention, opportunity, and viability. Throughout this stage, project stakeholders recognize the necessity of the project and assess its probable advantages and jeopardies. Important actions in the initiation stage contain performing a viability analysis, demarcating the plan's purposes, classifying stakeholders, and creating preliminary budgets and timelines. The chief deliverable of this stage is the project charter, which helps as a prescribed approval to originate the project.

The initiation stage is essential for guaranteeing that the venture associates with the establishment's tactical aims and offers a distinct understanding of what requires to be accomplished. It puts the platform for the succeeding stages and lays the foundation for effective project planning. Throughout this stage, project administrators and stakeholders cooperate to create a robust basis for productive project implementation. In this section, we will discover the implication of the project initiation stage, its important constituents, and the finest procedures for its application.

4.1.1 Importance of the Initiation Stage

The project initiation stage is repeatedly mentioned as the "front end" of a venture. It is during this stage that the project's viability, orientation with structural objectives, and probable menaces are evaluated. By bestowing time and endeavor to this stage, project executives can confirm that the project is tactically allied with the establishment's purposes and has a higher possibility of achievement. The project initiation stage offers the succeeding assistance:

Crucial Project Aims: Throughout project initiation, project supervisors function meticulously with stakeholders to distinctly outline project aims. This includes comprehending the anticipated consequences, deliverables, and accomplishment principles. Initiating definite purposes offers a strong course for the project team and confirms that everybody is operating in the direction of a shared ambition.

Evaluating Viability: The initiation stage permits project administrators to assess the venture's viability by counting several features for instance resource accessibility, budget restrictions, technological necessities, and legal and regulatory conformity. Evaluating practicability early on aids recognize possible obstructions and allows for appropriate alterations to the project strategy.

Classifying Stakeholders: Stakeholders perform an indispensable position in the accomplishment of a project. Throughout the initiation stage, project administrators recognize and involve crucial stakeholders, comprising patrons, consumers, end-users, and subject matter specialists. Through connecting stakeholders from the commencement, project executives may achieve valued understandings, amass necessities, and handle potentials efficiently.

Creating Project Authority: Efficient project authority is indispensable for project achievement. The initiation stage is an appropriate time to ascertain the project authority configuration, describe managerial procedures, and allocate tasks. This approves that functions and tasks are distinctly demarcated, interaction channels are created, and answerability is sustained throughout the project.

Estimating Risks: Identifying and managing risks is pivotal to project success. Throughout the initiation stage, project executives perform an initial risk assessment to identify possible intimidations and foster risk extenuation tactics. By tackling risks at the beginning, project executives can proactively handle them, lessening the possibility of adverse influences on the project.

4.1.2 Main Parts of the Initiation Stage

The project initiation stage usually comprises numerous crucial constituents that place the foundation for fruitful project implementation. These constituents can differ depending on the venture's intricacy and administrative necessities. Nevertheless, the succeeding elements are usually involved:

Project Charter: The project charter is an authorized document that outlines the venture's aims, opportunities, stakeholders, limitations, and accomplishment benchmarks. It aids as a reference position for project administrators and stakeholders, guaranteeing a common interpretation of the project's intention and track.

Stakeholder Recognition and Scrutiny: Recognizing and analyzing stakeholders is vital for effectual project management. This includes recognizing people or groups impacted by the project, comprehending their requirements and expectancies, and deciding their degree of effect and participation. Stakeholder scrutiny assists project administrators rank communication attempts and supervise stakeholder assignation during the project lifespan.

Viability Analysis: A viability analysis evaluates the project's feasibility, bearing in mind aspects such as technological possibility, financial feasibility, legal and regulatory amenability, and resource accessibility. It facilitates project administrators to decide whether the project is worth following and offers perceptions into probable jeopardies and challenges.

Project Opportunity Description: Describing the project opportunity comprises distinctly defining the limitations and deliverables of the venture. It assists handle opportunities and averts possibility creep, safeguarding that the project stays persistent

4.2 Planning Stage

The planning stage is where the venture's particulars are fleshed out and an all-inclusive strategy is established. This stage includes describing project necessities, forming a Work Breakdown Structure (WBS), assigning resources, and creating a genuine project timetable. Important actions throughout the planning stage contain classifying project purposes, characterizing project opportunities, performing stakeholder scrutiny, generating a project management strategy, and recognizing project risks. The principal deliverable of this stage is the project management strategy, which summarizes the tactic, procedures, and plans for implementing the project.

The planning stage enacts as a critical part of choosing the course for the venture and guaranteeing that all team associates are aligned with the project's ambitions and purposes. A clear strategy offers transparency, decreases doubt, and boosts the prospects of project accomplishment. This stage is described by all-inclusive evaluation, cautious decision-making, and punctilious preparation to confirm that the project has been prepared for accomplishment. In this section, we will explore several characteristics of the project planning stage, emphasizing vital considerations and the finest procedures for effectual project planning.

4.2.1 Identifying Purposes and Opportunity

The primary footstep in the project planning stage is to distinctly outline the project purposes and opportunities. This includes recognizing the venture's purpose, recognizing deliverables, and deciding the anticipated consequences. By expressing the purposes and possibilities, project executives can launch a well-defined direction for the venture and approve that all stakeholders have a shared recognition of the project's purposes.

4.2.2 Organizing Stakeholder Evaluation

Efficient project planning demands recognizing and investigating crucial stakeholders who will be impacted by or have an influence on the project. Stakeholders may comprise project sponsors, clients, team associates, end-users, and supervisory organizations. Knowing their expectancies, requirements, and apprehensions is vital for efficient communication, stakeholder engagement, and handling of probable risks and contradictions during the project lifespan.

4.2.3 Creating Work Breakdown Structure

A Work Breakdown Structure (WBS) is a tiered depiction of project responsibilities, deliverables, and sub-deliverables. It offers a graphic roadmap of the project, breaking down the work into controllable factors. The WBS enables resource apportionment, task allocation, and approximation of project timelines and budgets. It also supports recognizing dependencies between various project events, permitting successful scheduling and resource management.

4.2.4 Estimating Project Resources

Throughout the project planning stage, it is crucial to assess the resources essential to fulfill the project effectively. This comprises human resources, for instance, project team associates with precise skills and expertise, as well as physical resources, apparatus, and materials. Exact resource estimation supports in deciding project budgets, recognizing possible resource limitations, and confirming that the essential resources are accessible when wanted.

4.2.5 Creating Project Schedule

Generating an all-inclusive project schedule is a critical part of project planning. The timetable defines the order of project events, their duration, and interdependencies. It helps in recognizing critical path actions, which are indispensable for deciding the complete project duration. Project scheduling methods, such as the Critical Path Method (CPM) or the Program Evaluation and Review Technique (PERT), aid in improving project timelines, curtailing interruptions, and guaranteeing effectual resource employment.

4.2.6 Risk Evaluation and Mitigation

Risk estimation is a vital feature of the project planning stage. Classifying and scrutinizing probable risks and uncertainties permits project executives to create efficient risk extenuation tactics. Risk estimation includes organizing detailed scrutiny of internal and external features that could influence project achievement. It helps in ranking risks based on their chance and impression and framing suitable exigency strategies to abate their probable hostile consequences.

4.2.7 Founding Communication Networks

Efficient communication is essential for effective project implementation. Throughout the planning stage, project administrators must initiate unobstructed communication networks and distinguish the frequency and means of communication with stakeholders. This guarantees that project development, challenges, and updates are effectually communicated and stakeholders remain updated and involved during the project lifespan.

4.2.8 Specifying Control Systems

The planning stage is an appropriate period to launch procedures for project scrutinizing and control. This comprises stating Key Performance Indicators (KPIs) to assess project growth, beginning a project governance framework, and classifying informing arrangements. By setting up robust supervising and control apparatuses, project administrators can follow development, recognize divergences from the scheme, and take counteractive measures in a well-timed manner.

4.2.9 Creating a Change Management Plan

Change is an unavoidable portion of any project. Having a change management plan in place throughout the planning stage helps in efficiently supervising and regulating changes that can occur throughout project implementation. The strategy must define the procedure for assessing change requirements, evaluating their influence on the project, and getting compulsory consent before executing changes. A clear change management strategy warrants that project possibility is handled efficiently, curtailing scope creep and related risks.

4.2.10 Documenting Project Plan

Finally, it is critical to record the project strategy meticulously. The project plan functions as a reference record for all project stakeholders and offers a well-defined roadmap for project implementation. It must comprise all significant information, for example, project aims, opportunity, deliverables, timetables, resource distributions, risk organization policies, and communication tactics. A well-documented project strategy enables successful project control, improves stakeholder association, and allows efficient project implementation.

PROJECT MANAGEMENT

The project planning stage is a crucial phase in project management that sets the stage for effective project implementation. Utilizing cautious scrutiny, detailed preparation, and effectual communication, project administrators can lay a sound foundation for project accomplishment. Important concerns throughout the planning stage contain crucial project purposes and opportunities, performing stakeholder scrutiny, generating a work breakdown structure, assessing resources, creating a project timetable, evaluating risks, founding communication networks, identifying supervising and control methods, forming a change management strategy, and recording the project proposal. By addressing these matters, project administrators can strengthen the prospect of realizing project purposes, bringing quality consequences, and meeting stakeholder expectancies.

4.3 Execution Stage

The project execution stage is crucial in the life cycle of any project. It characterizes the realization of the project strategy and the conversion of concepts and perceptions into substantial deliverables. Throughout this stage, project teams function conscientiously to perform tasks, scrutinize development, manage resources, and eventually attain project purposes. In this section, we will offer an all-inclusive summary of the project execution stage, investigating its important components, challenges, and best practices.

Crucial components of the project execution stage are as follows:

4.3.1 Task Execution

Throughout this phase, project tasks and activities are executed by the project team members. This includes the allocation of resources, performing the necessary activities, and coordinating efforts to ensure smooth progress.

4.3.2 Resource Management

Effectual resource management is indispensable in the execution phase. Project executives must guarantee that the required resources, such as human resources, equipment, and materials, are obtainable and applied efficiently to complete tasks on time and within budget.

4.3.3 Growth Monitoring

Incessant supervision of project development is essential to identify potential issues, and deviations from the plan, and take corrective actions promptly. Project administrators employ various tools and techniques to track progress, such as progress reports, status meetings, and Key Performance Indicators (KPIs).

4.3.4 Communication and Teamwork

Open and efficient communication among project stakeholders is crucial during the execution stage. Project teams need to cooperate, exchange information, share updates, and settle issues swiftly to guarantee everyone is aligned and working towards a mutual purpose.

4.3.5 Risk Controlling

Recognizing and managing risks is a continuing procedure during project execution. Project administrators must proactively evaluate risks, implement risk mitigation policies, and monitor potential risks throughout the execution stage to curtail their effect on the project's accomplishment.

4.3.6 Quality Management

Upholding high-quality criteria is vital in the execution stage. Project teams should adhere to predefined quality standards, organize regular reviews, execute tests, and address any quality issues on time to guarantee that deliverables meet or exceed expectations.

4.3.7 Change Controlling

Change is unavoidable in projects, and the execution stage is no exception. Project administrators must be ready to handle change requests, assess their impact on the project, and implement suitable change management techniques to accommodate permitted changes without compromising project purposes.

4.3.8 Challenges

The project execution stage presents numerous challenges that project teams must address to guarantee fruitful project delivery. Some familiar challenges include:

Scope Creep

Unrestrained changes to the project scope can lead to scope creep, where additional requirements are added without proper evaluation or approval. This can result in increased costs, extended timelines, and reduced overall project success.

Resource Limitations

Inadequate accessibility of resources, such as budget, personnel, or equipment, can hamper project execution. Project teams must prudently manage resources, prioritize responsibilities, and optimize resource apportionment to mitigate the effect of constraints.

Team Alliance

Ensuring helpful association and synchronization among project team associates can be challenging, especially in large or geographically disseminated teams. Efficient communication networks, frequent meetings, and teamwork tools can support bridging the gap and fostering cooperation.

Stakeholder Expectancies

Handling stakeholder expectancies is vital during the project execution stage. Project administrators should uphold open lines of communication, impart consistent updates, and address anxieties to keep stakeholders informed and involved.

Risk Moderation

Identifying and mitigating risks is a lasting process throughout project implementation. Project teams must proactively assess risks, utilize contingency tactics, and frequently review and update risk management plans to diminish probable negative influences.

4.3.9 Lessons Learned

Unceasingly capture lessons learned through the project implementation stage. Record achievements, challenges, and best procedures to enable knowledge transfer and enrich future project implementation.

The project implementation stage is a crucial phase where project strategies are put into action, and project purposes are attained. By efficiently performing tasks, handling resources, monitoring development, and addressing challenges, project teams can boost the possibility of project accomplishment. Pursuing best practices, upholding effective interaction, nurturing teamwork, and welcoming adaptive tactics will contribute to effective project implementation and eventually deliver satisfactory consequences.

4.4 Scrutinizing and Control Stage

Efficient project management necessitates cautious planning, implementation, and control to guarantee the fruitful conclusion of a project. The project scrutinizing and control stage is a vital constituent of this procedure. It includes following project development, recognizing divergences from the strategy, applying remedial steps, and confirming that the project stays on track toward its objectives. In this section, we will investigate the project scrutinizing and control stage, deliberating its significance, crucial events, and best procedures.

Importance of Project Scrutinizing and Control

The project scrutinizing and control stage is vital for numerous causes. Firstly, it permits project administrators to evaluate the project's functioning against the defined purposes and deliverables. By carefully scrutinizing the project, executives can recognize any inconsistencies between the premeditated and real consequences, empowering them to take appropriate counteractive activities.

Secondly, project scrutinizing and control offers a system to trace the effectual application of project resources, together with time, budget, and human resources. By unceasingly appraising resource apportionment and consumption, project executives can classify fields of enhancement and optimize resource application, guaranteeing that the project remains within budget and timelines.

Thirdly, effectual project scrutinizing and control permit project stakeholders to remain updated about the project's development. Consistent reporting and communication channels guarantee that stakeholders have up-to-date information and can offer responses or make resolutions when required. This endorses transparency, responsibility, and stakeholder assignation during the project lifespan.

Crucial Actions in Project Scrutinizing and Control

The project scrutinizing and control stage includes numerous actions that contribute to the overall accomplishment of the venture. Let's look at some of the important actions involved:

4.4.1 Performance Evaluation and Recording

This activity includes evaluating project performance against predetermined metrics and sending frequent testimonies to stakeholders. Key Performance Indicators (KPIs) are created to assess development, for instance, cost alteration, timetable modification, and quality metrics. These details support stakeholders measure the project's condition and make informed judgments.

4.4.2 Risk Checking and Controlling

Risks are intrinsic in any venture, and supervising and managing them is vital for accomplishment. Throughout this stage, project executives uninterruptedly recognize, evaluate, and rank risks. They foster mitigation policies and exigency tactics to curtail the effect of possible risks. Consistent risk evaluations and updates confirm that risks are proactively tackled during the project lifespan.

4.4.3 Change Handling

Change is unavoidable in projects, and active change control is necessary for handling it. The scrutinizing and control stage comprises evaluating change requests, assessing their influences, and determining whether they align with project purposes. Change control boards or committees evaluate and authorize changes, guaranteeing that they are appropriately executed without destructively affecting the project's possibility, timetable, or budget.

4.4.4 Quality Assurance and Management

Delivering a high-grade product or service is a key objective of any venture. Quality assurance contains creating procedures and benchmarks to guarantee that project deliverables meet the mandatory quality standards. Quality control activities focus on inspecting project yields, recognizing imperfections or divergences, and employing counteractive activities to uphold or enrich quality.

4.4.5 Timetable and Cost Management

Scrutinizing project timetables and expenses is crucial for successful project management. Project executives follow actual progress against the premeditated timetable and budget, recognizing any discrepancies. They investigate the reasons for divergences and take counteractive measures, for instance, re-allocating resources or amending the schedule, to bring the venture back on track.

4.4.6 Culture of Constant Upgrading

Accenting a philosophy of unceasing development inspires project teams to recognize and execute better practices through the project lifecycle. Lessons learned from preceding projects are recorded and distributed, allowing teams to evade common pitfalls and improve their performance in upcoming activities.

The project scrutinizing and control stage is an essential stage in project management, assuring that projects stay on track, meet aims, and deliver the anticipated consequences. By carefully monitoring project performance, tracking resources, managing risks, and executing essential changes, project administrators can optimize project effectiveness and accomplishment.

Accepting best practices, such as creating well-defined objectives, expressing KPIs, nurturing efficient communication, and utilizing project management tools, improves the efficiency of the scrutinizing and control stage. Eventually, effectual project supervising and control contribute to the overall achievement of projects and permit establishments to attain their premeditated ambitions.

4.5 Closure Stage

Project closure is a vital stage in project management that denotes the conclusion of a project's lifespan. It includes the formal conclusion of all project activities, guaranteeing that the project purposes have been met, and enabling an easy transition to post-project processes. The closure stage is often ignored or undervalued, but it is critical for assessing project performance, capturing lessons learned, and tying up loose ends. This section investigates the implication of the project closure stage and emphasizes its important constituents and benefits.

Definition and Purpose

The project closure stage includes the actions, procedures, and measures undertaken to formally terminate a project. It intends to confirm that all project deliverables have been finished, stakeholders' expectancies have been met, and all required documentation and knowledge have been transferred. The closure stage aspires to attain project purposes, evaluate project performance, and offer a basis for forthcoming projects.

Important Components of the Closure Stage

4.5.1 Conclusion of Project Deliverables

The closure stage includes confirming that all project deliverables have been successfully created and accepted. This contains conducting final reviews, completing quality assurance inspections, and getting sign-offs from appropriate stakeholders.

4.5.2 Formal Acceptance

As soon as the project deliverables have been accomplished, the project administrator seeks official acceptance from the client or sponsor. This phase warrants that the project has met the agreed-upon requirements and has fulfilled the client's needs.

4.5.3 Transition Planning

Project closure contains preparation for the transition from project activities to post-project processes. This includes recognizing the resources, responsibilities, and processes essential for the ongoing maintenance, support, or application of the project's outcomes.

4.5.4 Documentation and Archiving

Another crucial element of the closure phase is the

documentation and archiving of project-related information. This comprises project plans, reports, agreements, lessons learned, and other related documentation. Appropriate archiving guarantees that valued project information is conserved and can be utilized as a reference for upcoming projects.

4.5.5 Stakeholder Communication

The closure stage necessitates efficient communication with all project stakeholders, including the client, team associates, and other related participants. It includes sharing project consequences, addressing any unsettled matters, and conveying gratitude for the stakeholders' involvement.

4.5.6 Financial Closure

Financial closure includes finalizing all financial aspects of the project, as well as reconciling unpaid invoices, closing accounts, and performing financial audits. It guarantees that all financial commitments and obligations associated with the venture are fulfilled.

4.5.7 Resource Reallocation

As projects terminate, resources, such as personnel, equipment, and budget, can be transferred to other projects or operative activities within the establishment. Successful closure allows for the economic utilization of resources and increases their potential worth.

4.5.8 Relationship Building

The closure stage offers a chance to assess client satisfaction and address any outstanding concerns or issues. By confirming that clients' expectations have been met, project closure reinforces the connection between the establishment and its clients, boosting the prospects of upcoming alliances.

4.5.9 Learning and Incessant Upgrading

The closure stage contributes to organizational learning by nurturing a philosophy of constant development. By methodically recording lessons learned and integrating them into project management exercises, establishments can improve their project delivery competencies, curtail risks, and optimize upcoming project consequences.

4.5.10 Legal and Contractual Closure

Project closure involves ensuring legal and contractual compliance, for instance finishing agreements, resolving legal disputes, and releasing liabilities. Appropriate closure reduces the establishment's exposure to legal risks and defends its reputation.

4.5.11 Challenges

Stakeholder Disengagement

As projects near the finishing point, stakeholders may start to disengage, which can lead to incomplete documentation, unsettled matters, or an absence of backing throughout the closure stage. Project administrators must proactively communicate and involve stakeholders to ensure their continued engagement until the project's formal closure.

Knowledge Transfer

Shifting project knowledge to appropriate parties, including operational teams or upcoming project teams, can be challenging. Project closure must comprise an all-inclusive information handover strategy, guaranteeing that significant project understandings and documentation are efficiently transferred and made available to those who require them.

Emotional Impact

Project closure can arouse a range of emotions among project team associates, including a sense of loss, relief, or even doubt about upcoming assignments. Project executives must provide assistance and acknowledgment to team associates, recognizing their roles and enabling an effortless shift to different projects or roles.

Closure Criteria

Specifying clear-cut closure norms at the commencement of a project is important. These norms must define the precise circumstances that should be met for the project to be deemed effectively concluded. Definite closure conditions offer simplicity and help in deciding when it is suitable to instigate the closure stage.

The project closure stage is a vital phase in the project management lifespan that should not be ignored. It confirms that project purposes have been met, stakeholders are contented, and valued knowledge is gained for future use. By finishing all project activities, assessing execution, and tying up loose ends, establishments can improve their project delivery proficiencies, promote the relentless enhancement, and construct sturdier relations with clients. Appropriately implemented project closure leads to lucrative project consequences, smooth changeovers, and increased organizational effectiveness.

4.6 Iterative Stages

The iterative stage is a vital constituent of the project management procedure that focuses on the constant development and improvement of project deliverables. It includes reiterating cycles of preparation, execution, and assessment to improve project consequences and adjust to altering necessities. The iterative stage is predominantly prominent in agile project management procedures, for instance, in Scrum and Kanban, where it shapes the basis of project implementation.

Throughout the iterative stage, the project team acts collaboratively to break down the project into smaller, manageable augmentations named iterations or sprints. Each repetition usually lasts for a fixed period, for instance, two weeks, and aims to produce a tangible and functioning deliverable. The iterative method allows for elasticity and authorizes teams to answer to feedback, as well as disparities, and continually improve the venture's track.

One of the significant advantages of the reiterative stage is the competence to accumulate preliminary feedback and understanding from stakeholders. By delivering working prototypes or deliverables at the end of each repetition, project teams can dynamically include stakeholders and obtain their endeavor. This response loop ensures that the project stays allied with stakeholders' expectations and allows for indispensable modifications and enhancements. It also reduces the risks associated with delivering a final product that does not meet the stakeholders' necessities.

Additionally, the iterative phase allows teams to address insecurities and mitigate risks during the project lifespan. By breaking the project into smaller iterations, teams can rapidly recognize and address possible issues before they intensify. Consistent assessment and review sessions offer chances to examine the project's development, find areas for enhancement, and make essential alterations to following iterations. This iterative feedback loop allows for appropriate risk mitigation and improves the overall quality of project consequences.

Another substantial benefit of the iterative stage is the capability to adjust to shifting requirements and market circumstances. In today's fast-paced commercial situation, project requirements frequently change as new information becomes accessible or as market dynamics amend. The iterative method recognizes this realism and delivers a framework for adopting transformation. Through recurrent reiterations, project teams can integrate new necessities, regulate priorities, and pivot their policies to remain receptive to market demands.

Furthermore, the iterative phase endorses teamwork and clarity within the project team. By working in short reiterations, team associates have consistent chances to interconnect, share advancement, and synchronize their efforts. This alliance nurtures a perception of proprietorship and cooperative accountability, leading to augmented team interconnection and thruput. It also allows team associates to influence their assorted perceptions and proficiency, resulting in state-of-the-art resolutions and enhanced decision-making.

To efficiently perform the iterative phase, project teams

utilize numerous apparatuses and procedures. Agile project management procedures offer frameworks such as Scrum, which contains regular stand-up meetings, backlog refinement assemblies, and sprint planning sessions. These tools enable successful communication, task prioritization, and iterative progress. Moreover, project management software, such as Jira or Trello, can be applied to follow and control iterations, responsibilities, and development.

In conclusion, the iterative stage is an indispensable phase in the project management procedure that permits incessant development, adaptation, and risk mitigation. By breaking the plan into minor repetitions and releasing tangible deliverables, teams can collect primary feedback from stakeholders, address insecurities, and make essential modifications. The iterative tactic endorses alliance, clarity, and receptiveness leading to improved project consequences and upgraded stakeholder satisfaction. As industries continue to navigate an ever-changing landscape, accepting the iterative stage is imperative for fruitful project implementation and attaining optimal outcomes.

4.7 Conclusion

Project management encompasses numerous distinct stages, each playing a decisive role in the fruitful accomplishment of a project. The initiation stage sets the foundation for the project, the planning stage offers a roadmap, the execution stage brings the strategy to life, the monitoring and control stage guarantees adherence to the strategy, and the closure stage wraps up the venture and captures valued lessons learned.

By comprehending and efficiently managing each stage, project administrators can enhance the probability of project accomplishment, meet stakeholder expectancies, and deliver high-quality results. The project management procedure is iterative, and dynamic, and necessitates incessant monitoring, revision, and effectual communication. With an organized tactic and a focus on each stage, project administrators can navigate challenges, mitigate risks, and attain project purposes within the demarcated restrictions.

4.8 Algorithm for Software

Initialize the Project Management Software:

Create necessary data structures and variables to store projects, tasks, and users.

Load existing data from a database or file, if applicable.

User Authentication:

Prompt the user for login credentials (username and password).

Validate the credentials against a user database.

Grant access to the software if the credentials are valid.

Handle authentication errors and provide appropriate feedback.

Main Menu Loop:

Display the main menu options to the user.

Accept user input for the chosen menu option.

Based on the selected option, execute the corresponding functionality.

Create a New Project:

Prompt the user for project details such as name, description, start date, and end date.

Create a new project object with the provided details.

Add the project to the list of projects.

View Existing Projects:

Display a list of existing projects, including their names and
statuses.

Allow the user to select a project to view more details.

Project Actions Menu:

Display project-specific menu options to the user.

Accept user input for the chosen action.

Based on the selected option, execute the corresponding
functionality.

Create a New Task:

Prompt the user for task details such as name, description,
start date, and end date.

Create a new task object with the provided details.

Add the task to the selected project's task list.

View Project Details:

Display the selected project's details, including tasks, start
date, end date, and progress.

Allow the user to select a task for more detailed
information.

Update Task Status:

Prompt the user to select a task to update its status.

Mark the selected task as completed or update its progress.

Update the project's overall progress based on task
completion.

Delete a Task:

Prompt the user to select a task to delete.
Remove the selected task from the project's task list.

Save and Exit:

Save all the data (projects, tasks, etc.) to a database or file
for future use.
Display a farewell message.
Exit the program.

This is a high-level algorithm plan that offers an impression of the main steps and functionalities of project management software. You can develop upon these steps, add error handling, implement data perseverance, and include extra features based on your precise necessities.

4.9 Sample Codes in Java

Project Class:

```java
public class Project {
    private String name;
    private String description;
    private Date startDate;
    private Date endDate;
    private List<Task> tasks;

    // Constructors, getters, and setters

    public void addTask(Task task) {
        tasks.add(task);
    }

    public void removeTask(Task task) {
        tasks.remove(task);
    }

    // Other project-related methods
}
```

Task Class:

```java
public class Task {
    private String name;
    private String description;
    private Date startDate;
    private Date endDate;
    private boolean completed;
```

```java
    // Constructors, getters, and setters

    public void markAsCompleted() {
        completed = true;
    }

    // Other task-related methods
}
```

User Class:

```java
public class User {
    private String username;
    private String password;
    private List<Project> projects;

    // Constructors, getters, and setters

    public void createProject(String name, String description,
Date startDate, Date endDate) {
        Project project = new Project(name, description,
startDate, endDate);
        projects.add(project);
    }

    public void deleteProject(Project project) {
        projects.remove(project);
    }

    // Other user-related methods
}
```

Main Class (Entry Point):

```java
import java.util.Scanner;

public class Main {
    public static void main(String[] args) {
        // Initialize variables and objects

        Scanner scanner = new Scanner(System.in);

        // User authentication logic

        // Main menu
        while (true) {
            // Display menu options

            int choice = scanner.nextInt();

            switch (choice) {
                case 1:
                    // Create a new project
                    break;
                case 2:
                    // View existing projects
                    break;
                case 3:
                    // Select a project and perform actions
                    break;
                case 4:
                    // Exit the program
                    scanner.close();
                    System.exit(0);
                    break;
```

```
        default:
            System.out.println("Invalid choice. Please try
again.");
            break;
        }
      }
    }
}
```

This code offers a rudimentary structure for project management software, with classes for projects, tasks, and users. It also contains a simple main class that handles user authentication and presents a menu for several processes.

Keep in mind that this is just a preliminary point, and you will need to improve the code with other functionalities like data persistence, user input authentication, task assignment, warnings, and more.

4.10 Sample Code in C

```c
#include <stdio.h>
#include <stdlib.h>
#include <string.h>

#define MAX_TASKS 100

// Structure for a task
typedef struct {
    char description[100];
    char due_date[20];
    int completed;
} Task;

// Structure for a project
typedef struct {
    char name[50];
    Task tasks[MAX_TASKS];
    int num_tasks;
} Project;

// Function to add a new task to a project
void addTask(Project *project) {
    if (project->num_tasks >= MAX_TASKS) {
        printf("Maximum number of tasks reached for this project.\n");
        return;
    }

    Task *task = &project->tasks[project->num_tasks];
```

```
    printf("Enter task description: ");
    fgets(task->description, sizeof(task->description), stdin);
    task->description[strcspn(task->description,  "\n")]  =
'\0'; // Remove trailing newline

    printf("Enter task due date: ");
    fgets(task->due_date, sizeof(task->due_date), stdin);
    task->due_date[strcspn(task->due_date, "\n")]  =  '\0';
// Remove trailing newline

    task->completed = 0;

    project->num_tasks++;
}

// Function to mark a task as completed
void completeTask(Project *project) {
    int task_num;

    printf("Enter task number to mark as completed: ");
    scanf("%d", &task_num);
    getchar(); // Consume newline character

    if (task_num < 1 || task_num > project->num_tasks) {
        printf("Invalid task number.\n");
        return;
    }

    Task *task = &project->tasks[task_num - 1];
    task->completed = 1;
}
```

```c
// Function to print project details
void printProject(const Project *project) {
    printf("Project: %s\n", project->name);
    printf("Tasks:\n");

    for (int i = 0; i < project->num_tasks; i++) {
        const Task *task = &project->tasks[i];
        printf("%d. Description: %s\n", i + 1, task->description);
        printf("  Due date: %s\n", task->due_date);
        printf("        Status: %s\n", task->completed ? "Completed" : "Incomplete");
    }
}

int main() {
    Project *project = (Project *)malloc(sizeof(Project));

    printf("Enter project name: ");
    fgets(project->name, sizeof(project->name), stdin);
    project->name[strcspn(project->name, "\n")] = '\0'; // Remove trailing newline

    project->num_tasks = 0;

    int choice;

    do {
        printf("\n--- Project Management Menu ---\n");
        printf("1. Add task\n");
        printf("2. Mark task as completed\n");
        printf("3. Print project details\n");
```

```c
        printf("4. Exit\n");
        printf("Enter your choice: ");
        scanf("%d", &choice);
        getchar(); // Consume newline character

        switch (choice) {
            case 1:
                addTask(project);
                break;
            case 2:
                completeTask(project);
                break;
            case 3:
                printProject(project);
                break;
            case 4:
                printf("Exiting program.\n");
                break;
            default:
                printf("Invalid choice. Please try again.\n");
        }
    } while (choice != 4);

    free(project);

    return 0;
}
```

4.11 Sample Code in Python

```python
projects = {}

def create_project():
    project_name = input("Enter project name: ")
    project_description = input("Enter project description: ")
    projects[project_name] = project_description
    print("Project created successfully!")

def view_projects():
    if not projects:
        print("No projects found.")
    else:
        print("Projects:")
        for project_name, project_description in projects.items():
            print(f"Name: {project_name}")
            print(f"Description: {project_description}")
            print("-" * 20)

def delete_project():
    project_name = input("Enter project name to delete: ")
    if project_name in projects:
        del projects[project_name]
        print("Project deleted successfully!")
    else:
        print("Project not found.")

def menu():
    print("Welcome to the Project Management System!")
```

```python
print("1. Create a new project")
print("2. View all projects")
print("3. Delete a project")
print("4. Exit")
choice = input("Enter your choice (1-4): ")

if choice == "1":
    create_project()
elif choice == "2":
    view_projects()
elif choice == "3":
    delete_project()
elif choice == "4":
    exit()
else:
    print("Invalid choice. Please try again.")

while True:
    menu()
```

This program permits you to accomplish the following actions:

1. Create a new project by providing a name and description.
2. View all existing projects along with their names and descriptions.
3. Delete a project by entering its name.
4. Exit the program.

You can develop this elementary structure to add more functionalities or improve the user interface as needed.

4.12 Sample Code for MATLAB

```
function projectManagement()

    % Number of tasks in the project
    numTasks = input('Enter the number of tasks: ');

    % Initialize task array
    tasks = cell(numTasks, 1);

    % Task names and durations
    for i = 1:numTasks
        tasks{i}.name = input(sprintf('Enter the name of task
%d: ', i), 's');
        tasks{i}.duration = input(sprintf('Enter the duration
of task %d (in days): ', i));
    end

    % Task dependencies
    for i = 1:numTasks
        dependentTasks = input(sprintf('Enter the dependent
tasks for task %d (separated by spaces, 0 if none): ', i));
        tasks{i}.dependencies                        =
dependentTasks(dependentTasks > 0);
    end

    % Calculate project duration and critical path
    [projectDuration,          criticalPath]         =
calculateCriticalPath(tasks);

    % Display results
    fprintf('\nProject        duration:      %d      days\n',
```

```
projectDuration);
    fprintf('Critical path: ');
    for i = 1:length(criticalPath)
        fprintf('%s ', tasks{criticalPath(i)}.name);
    end
    fprintf('\n');

end

function [projectDuration, criticalPath] = calculateCriticalPath(tasks)
    % Number of tasks
    numTasks = length(tasks);

    % Initialize earliest start and finish times
    earliestStart = zeros(numTasks, 1);
    earliestFinish = zeros(numTasks, 1);

    % Calculate the earliest start and finish times for each task
    for i = 1:numTasks
        if isempty(tasks{i}.dependencies)
            earliestStart(i) = 0;
        else
            dependencyTimes = earliestFinish(tasks{i}.dependencies);
            earliestStart(i) = max(dependencyTimes);
        end
        earliestFinish(i) = earliestStart(i) + tasks{i}.duration;
    end

    % Initialize the latest start and finish times
```

```
    latestStart = earliestStart;
    latestFinish = earliestFinish;

    % Calculate the latest start and finish times for each task
    for i = numTasks:-1:1
        if isempty(tasks{i}.dependencies)
            latestFinish(i) = earliestFinish(i);
        else
            dependencyTimes                              =
    latestStart(tasks{i}.dependencies);
            latestFinish(i) = min(dependencyTimes);
        end
        latestStart(i) = latestFinish(i) - tasks{i}.duration;
    end

    % Calculate slack for each task
    slack = latestStart - earliestStart;

    % Find critical path tasks
    criticalPathIndices = find(slack == 0);

    % Calculate project duration
    projectDuration = max(latestFinish);

    % Store critical path task indices
    criticalPath = [];
    for i = 1:length(criticalPathIndices)
        criticalPath    =    [criticalPath    findCriticalPath(tasks,
    criticalPathIndices(i))];
    end

    % Sort critical path tasks in order
```

```matlab
    criticalPath = sort(criticalPath);

end

function path = findCriticalPath(tasks, taskIndex)
    % Recursive function to find the critical path

    if isempty(tasks{taskIndex}.dependencies)
        path = taskIndex;
    else
        path = [taskIndex];
        for i = 1:length(tasks{taskIndex}.dependencies)
            path = [path findCriticalPath(tasks, tasks{taskIndex}.dependencies(i))];
        end
    end

end
```

To use this program, save it in a MATLAB file with a ".m" extension (e.g., "project_management.m") and run it in the MATLAB command window. The program will prompt you to enter the number of tasks, task names, durations, and dependencies. After that, it will calculate the project duration and critical path and display the results.

Please note that this is a basic example, and many other features of project management can be merged into a more inclusive program.

4.13 Exercise

1. What are the significant components of project initiation, and why is it vital to have a clear project initiation stage?

2. How do you recognize and analyze project stakeholders during the project planning phase?

3. What methods can be employed to efficiently define project scope and manage scope changes during the project?

4. How do you generate an accurate project schedule, and what factors should be considered when estimating project durations?

5. What are some common risk management techniques used during the project execution stage, and how do they help mitigate project risks?

6. How do you successfully monitor and control project progress, and what tools or metrics can be utilized to track project performance?

7. What approaches can be utilized to manage project team dynamics and ensure effective communication and

collaboration among team members?

8. How do you approach procurement and vendor management during the project implementation phase?

9. What are some best practices for conducting project reviews and lessons-learned sessions at the end of a project?

10. How do you close out a project effectively, including tasks such as finalizing project deliverables, conducting project evaluations, and transitioning project outcomes to the appropriate stakeholders?

5 Project Initiation

5.1 Weighted Decision Matrix

The project initiation stage is a vital phase in any project's life cycle. It includes classifying the project's purposes, scope, and stakeholders, as well as deciding its viability and aligning it with the establishment's strategic goals. One effective tool that can aid in the decision-making procedure throughout the project initiation stage is a weighted decision matrix.

A weighted decision matrix, also identified as a decision matrix scrutiny or decision-making grid, is a structured method that permits project directors and teams to assess and compare several alternatives or options based on numerous conditions. By allocating weights to each criterion and ranking each alternative against those standards, a weighted decision matrix proposes a methodical and objective framework for decision-making.

The primary step in generating a weighted decision matrix is to recognize the applicable criteria. These criteria must be precise, quantifiable, and aligned with the project's objectives and ideas. For instance, if the project contains choosing a new software vendor, the conditions might contain cost, functionality, scalability, customer support, and ease of integration.

Once the measures are acknowledged, the subsequent step

is to allocate weights to each criterion based on their comparative rank. The weights specify the worth of each criterion in attaining the project's objectives. The sum of all weights must equal 100%, guaranteeing that the assessment is practical and complete.

After allotting weights, the project team assesses each alternative or choice against the criteria and allocates a score or rating for every condition. The scores are typically based on a numerical scale, such as 1 to 5 or 1 to 10, with higher values indicating improved performance or alignment with the criterion. The assessment procedure can contain separate evaluations or collective deliberations within the project team or pertinent stakeholders.

When all alternatives are assessed against the criteria and scored, the following step is to compute the weighted scores. This is performed by multiplying each score by its corresponding weight and summing up the results. The weighted scores offer a quantitative depiction of how well every substitute meets the project's necessities and purposes.

Lastly, the project team can scrutinize the consequences of the weighted decision matrix to make informed decisions. The alternative with the maximum weighted score is normally considered the most advantageous option. Though, the project team must also contemplate other aspects, such as budget constraints, resource availability, and risk factors, before making a concluding decision.

The benefits of employing a weighted decision matrix throughout the project initiation stage are abundant. Firstly, it offers a clear and organized approach to decision-making, disregarding prejudices and subjective decisions. The usage of predefined criteria and weights confirms that decisions are based on objective valuations and align with the project's strategic objectives.

Secondly, a weighted decision matrix enables communication and teamwork among project stakeholders. Connecting related stakeholders in the assessment procedure stimulates a collective interpretation of the project's necessities and nurtures a sense of proprietorship and engagement.

Furthermore, a weighted decision matrix benefits project teams to handle the intricacy and control of numerous alternatives concurrently. It permits a methodical assessment of diverse possibilities, letting project executives appraise their strengths, weaknesses, and trade-offs.

Moreover, the usage of a weighted decision matrix enhances the traceability of decisions. The documented assessment procedure offers a clear justification for the nominated alternative, which can be beneficial for future reference or audits.

Though, it is important to recognize the restrictions of a

weighted decision matrix. The accuracy of the consequences depends on the worth of the criteria, weights, and scores allocated. If the conditions are not well-defined or the weights are not appropriately standardized, the consequences may be prejudiced or deceptive.

Additionally, a weighted decision matrix must not be the only basis of a project's course. It is an instrument that helps decision-making, but other features for example expert judgment, market research, and feasibility studies must also be taken into account.

To put it briefly, a weighted decision matrix is a valued instrument for the project initiation stage. It empowers project administrators and teams to appraise and contrast substitutes factually, based on predefined standards and their comparative significance. By encouraging transparency, alliance, and knowledgeable decision-making, a weighted decision matrix contributes to the fruitful initiation of projects and aligns them with administrative ambitions.

5.1.1 Weighted Decision Matrix Usage

A Weighted Decision Matrix (WDM) is a valued tool in project management that helps evaluate and grade numerous possibilities or substitutes based on specific norms. It allows project teams to make knowledgeable decisions by conveying weights to each criterion and scoring each option against those criteria. This process ensures that decisions are based on objective assessments rather than subjective opinions.

In the Project Initiation Phase, which is the initial phase of a project's life cycle, critical decisions need to be made to define the project's scope, objectives, and feasibility. A WDM can be used to measure different project options and select the most viable one. Let's consider a sample scenario where a corporation is planning to present a new product line, and the project initiation team needs to choose between three options: Option A, Option B, and Option C. The team will assess these options based on criteria such as market demand, financial viability, and technical feasibility.

Step 1: State Criteria
The first step in creating a WDM is to identify the relevant criteria for evaluation. In this example, we will consider the following criteria:
1. Market Demand: Assessing the potential customer demand for the product.
2. Financial Viability: Evaluating the profitability and return on investment.
3. Technical Feasibility: Examining the company's

capabilities to develop and manufacture the product.

4. Resources Required: Analyzing the resources (financial, human, and infrastructure) needed for each option.

5. Timeframe: Considering the time required to develop and launch the product.

Step 2: Allocate Weights

The project initiation team needs to assign weights to each criterion to reflect its relative importance. The sum of all weights should be equal to 1. Let's assume the team assigns the following weights:

1. Market Demand: 0.3
2. Financial Viability: 0.2
3. Technical Feasibility: 0.2
4. Resources Required: 0.15
5. Timeframe: 0.15

The weights indicate that the team considers market demand as the most critical criterion, followed by financial viability and technical feasibility. The resources required and timeframe are considered slightly less important in this evaluation.

Step 3: Grading the Options

Next, the team will score each option against each criterion. The scoring can be done on a scale of, for example, 1 to 5, where 1 represents poor performance and 5 represents excellent performance.

Option A:

- Market Demand: 4
- Financial Viability: 3
- Technical Feasibility: 4
- Resources Required: 2
- Timeframe: 3

Option B:
- Market Demand: 5
- Financial Viability: 4
- Technical Feasibility: 3
- Resources Required: 4
- Timeframe: 3

Option C:
- Market Demand: 3
- Financial Viability: 5
- Technical Feasibility: 5
- Resources Required: 3
- Timeframe: 4

Step 4: Compute Scores

To calculate the weighted scores for each option, we multiply the score of each criterion by its corresponding weight and sum the results. Let's calculate the weighted scores for each option:

Option A:
- Market Demand: 4 * 0.3 = 1.2
- Financial Viability: 3 * 0.2 = 0.6
- Technical Feasibility: 4 * 0.2 = 0.8
- Resources Required: 2 * 0.15 = 0.3

- Timeframe: 3 * 0.15 = 0.45

Weighted Score for Option A = 1.2 + 0.6 + 0.8 + 0.3 + 0.45 = 3.35

Option B:
- Market Demand: 5 * 0.3 = 1.5
- Financial Viability: 4 * 0.2 = 0.8
- Technical Feasibility: 3 * 0.2 = 0.6
- Resources Required: 4 * 0.15 = 0.6
- Timeframe: 3 * 0.15 = 0.45

Weighted Score for Option B = 1.5 + 0.8 + 0.6 + 0.6 + 0.45 = 4.05

Option C:
- Market Demand: 3 * 0.3 = 0.9
- Financial Viability: 5 * 0.2 = 1.0
- Technical Feasibility: 5 * 0.2 = 1.0
- Resources Required: 3 * 0.15 = 0.45
- Timeframe: 4 * 0.15 = 0.6

Weighted Score for Option C = 0.9 + 1.0 + 1.0 + 0.45 + 0.6 = 3.95

Step 5: Assess and Select the Favored Option
By comparing the weighted scores, the team can identify the option that performs the best overall. In this example, Option B has the highest weighted score (4.05), followed closely by Option C (3.95), and then Option A (3.35). Based on the evaluation, the team would consider Option B as the

most favorable choice for the new product line

Step 6: Review and Decision

Once the evaluation is complete, it is crucial to review the results and consider any additional factors that may influence the decision. The project initiation team should discuss the outcomes, assess the risks associated with the preferred option, and make a final decision.

It's important to note that a WDM is just one tool in the decision-making process. Other considerations, such as stakeholder input, risk analysis, and strategic alignment, should also be taken into account. Furthermore, the weights and scores assigned to the criteria are subjective and can vary based on the project and organizational context.

In conclusion, a Weighted Decision Matrix is a valued technique during the Project Initiation Phase as it helps project teams evaluate and prioritize various options based on specific criteria. By assigning weights to each criterion and scoring each option, the team can make informed and objective decisions. However, it is vital to remember that the WDM is just one component of the decision-making process and should be used in conjunction with other tools and considerations to ensure the best outcome for the project.

5.1.2 WDM Algorithm

Inputs:
- Criteria: A list of criteria for evaluating alternatives.
- Alternatives: A list of alternatives to be evaluated.
- Weights: A list of weights corresponding to the importance of each criterion. The weights should be normalized so that their sum is 1.
- Scores: A matrix representing the scores of each alternative for each criterion. Each row corresponds to an alternative, and each column corresponds to a criterion.

Output:
- Rankings: A list of alternatives ranked based on their overall scores.

Algorithm:
1. Initialize an empty dictionary called "overall_scores" to store the overall scores for each alternative.
2. For each alternative in the list of alternatives:
   - Initialize a variable called "overall_score" to 0.
   - For each criterion in the list of criteria:
   - Multiply the score of the alternative for the criterion by the weight of the criterion.
   - Add the result to the overall_score.
   - Store the overall_score for the alternative in the "overall_scores" dictionary, using the alternative as the key.
3. Sort the "overall_scores" dictionary in descending order based on the values (overall scores).
4. Extract the keys (alternatives) from the sorted "overall_scores" dictionary and store them in a list called "rankings".
5. Return the "rankings" list as the output.

5.1.3 Python Code

```
criteria = ['Cost', 'Quality', 'Delivery']
alternatives = ['Alternative 1', 'Alternative 2', 'Alternative 3']
weights = [0.4, 0.3, 0.3]
scores = [
  [0.8, 0.9, 0.7],
  [0.6, 0.7, 0.8],
  [0.7, 0.8, 0.9]
]

rankings = weighted_decision_matrix(criteria, alternatives,
weights, scores)
print(rankings)
```

Output:

```
['Alternative 2', 'Alternative 3', 'Alternative 1']
```

In the sample, 'Alternatives 2' has the maximum overall score according to the weighted decision matrix algorithm.

5.1.4 JAVA code

```java
import java.util.Scanner;

public class WeightedDecisionMatrix {
  public static void main(String[] args) {
    Scanner input = new Scanner(System.in);

    // Enter the number of options
    System.out.print("Enter the number of options: ");
    int numOptions = input.nextInt();

    // Enter the number of criteria
    System.out.print("Enter the number of criteria: ");
    int numCriteria = input.nextInt();

    // Create the matrix to store the scores
    double[][]          matrix          =          new
double[numOptions][numCriteria];

    // Enter the scores for each option and criterion
    for (int i = 0; i < numOptions; i++) {
      System.out.println("Enter the scores for option " +
(i + 1) + ":");
      for (int j = 0; j < numCriteria; j++) {
        System.out.print("Criterion " + (j + 1) + ": ");
        matrix[i][j] = input.nextDouble();
      }
      System.out.println();
    }

    // Enter the weights for each criterion
    double[] weights = new double[numCriteria];
    System.out.println("Enter    the    weights    for    each
criterion:");
```

```java
for (int i = 0; i < numCriteria; i++) {
    System.out.print("Criterion " + (i + 1) + ": ");
    weights[i] = input.nextDouble();
}

// Calculate the weighted scores
double[] weightedScores = new double[numOptions];
for (int i = 0; i < numOptions; i++) {
    double weightedSum = 0;
    for (int j = 0; j < numCriteria; j++) {
        weightedSum += matrix[i][j] * weights[j];
    }
    weightedScores[i] = weightedSum;
}

// Print the results
System.out.println("\nWeighted Scores:");
for (int i = 0; i < numOptions; i++) {
    System.out.println("Option " + (i + 1) + ": " +
weightedScores[i]);
    }
  }
}
```

This code permits you to enter the number of options and criteria for the decision matrix. Then, it prompts you to enter the scores for each option and criterion. After that, you can input the weights for each criterion. Lastly, the code calculates the weighted scores for each option and displays the results.

Please notice that this code accepts the input values are valid and does not include extensive error handling. You may want to add appropriate input validation and exception handling as per your requirements.

5.1.5 C Code

```c
#include <stdio.h>

#define MAX_ROWS 10
#define MAX_COLUMNS 10

void calculateWeightedSum(int
matrix[MAX_ROWS][MAX_COLUMNS], float
weights[MAX_COLUMNS], int numRows, int numCols,
float result[MAX_ROWS]) {
    for (int i = 0; i < numRows; i++) {
        float sum = 0.0;
        for (int j = 0; j < numCols; j++) {
            sum += matrix[i][j] * weights[j];
        }
        result[i] = sum;
    }
}

int main() {
    int matrix[MAX_ROWS][MAX_COLUMNS] = {
        {1, 2, 3},
        {4, 5, 6},
        {7, 8, 9}
    };

    float weights[MAX_COLUMNS] = {0.2, 0.3, 0.5};

    int numRows = 3;
    int numCols = 3;

    float result[MAX_ROWS];

    calculateWeightedSum(matrix, weights, numRows,
```

numCols, result);

```
    printf("Weighted Sum:\n");
    for (int i = 0; i < numRows; i++) {
        printf("%.2f\n", result[i]);
    }

    return 0;
}
```

In this instance, the `calculateWeightedSum` function takes a matrix, an array of weights, the number of rows and columns in the matrix, and an array to store the weighted sums. It computes the weighted sum for each row by multiplying each element in the row with its corresponding weight and summing the results. The resulting weighted sums are stored in the `result` array.

In the `main` function, we have defined a sample matrix, weights, and the number of rows and columns. We then call the `calculateWeightedSum` function and print the resulting weighted sums.

Note: In this sample, the matrix and weights are hardcoded for simplicity. You can modify the code to read input from the user or a file, depending on your requirements.

5.1.6 MATLAB Code

```
% Define the options and criteria
options = {'Option 1', 'Option 2', 'Option 3'};
criteria = {'Criterion 1', 'Criterion 2', 'Criterion 3', 'Criterion
4'};

% Define the weights for each criterion
weights = [0.3, 0.2, 0.4, 0.1];

% Initialize the decision matrix
decisionMatrix = zeros(length(options), length(criteria));

% Fill in the decision matrix with scores for each option and
criterion
% For simplicity, let's assume the scores are random
for i = 1:length(options)
   for j = 1:length(criteria)
      decisionMatrix(i, j) = randi([1, 10]);
   end
end

% Normalize the decision matrix
normalizedMatrix = decisionMatrix ./ sum(decisionMatrix);

% Calculate the weighted scores
weightedScores = normalizedMatrix * weights';

% Display the decision matrix and weighted scores
disp('Decision Matrix:');
disp(decisionMatrix);
disp('Normalized Matrix:');
disp(normalizedMatrix);
disp('Weighted Scores:');
disp(weightedScores);
```

```
% Find the best option based on the weighted scores
[~, bestOptionIndex] = max(weightedScores);
bestOption = options{bestOptionIndex};
disp(['Best Option: ', bestOption]);
```

In this code, we have described the options and criteria as cell arrays. Then, we have specified the weights for each criterion. Next, we have initialized the decision matrix as a matrix of zeros. We have iterated through each option and criterion to fill in the decision matrix with scores (you can replace the random scores with your evaluation technique).

After that, we normalized the decision matrix by dividing each element by the sum of the corresponding column. Then, we calculated the weighted scores by multiplying the normalized matrix with the weights vector.

Lastly, we have displayed the decision matrix, normalized matrix, and weighted scores. We have found the best option by locating the index of the maximum value in the weighted scores and retrieving the corresponding option. The best option is then displayed.

Note that this code assumes equal rank for each criterion. If you have a different set of weights, you can adjust the `weights` vector consequently.

5.2 Payback Period

The payback period is a vital financial metric used in the project initiation stage. It measures the time essential to recover the initial investment in a project through the net cash flows it creates. The significance of the payback period lies in its capability to offer a valued understanding of the viability, profitability, and risk associated with a project. This section will explore the implication of the payback period and its function in the project initiation stage.

One of the main benefits of calculating the payback period is its capacity to assess the project's financial viability. By deciding how long it takes for an investment to pay for itself, organizations can evaluate whether the project is worth pursuing. Projects with shorter payback periods are generally preferred as they offer quicker returns on investment, reducing the organization's exposure to financial risks. On the other hand, longer payback periods may show a higher level of uncertainty and probable financial strain.

The payback period also aids establishments to prioritize projects by providing a simple comparison tool. When faced with multiple project proposals, decision-makers can use the payback period to rank and select the most promising ones. By considering the time it takes to recover the initial investment, organizations can allocate their limited resources to projects that offer shorter payback periods, ensuring more efficient use of capital.

Besides, the payback period aids in assessing and managing project risk. Longer payback periods can designate a higher level of risk, as there is more uncertainty regarding the project's ability to generate adequate cash flows within a reasonable timeframe. By understanding the payback period, organizations can evaluate the associated risks and implement risk mitigation strategies accordingly. This might involve adjusting the project scope, timeline, or financial structure to minimize potential losses.

Moreover, the payback period assists in decision-making throughout the project initiation stage. It serves as a benchmark against which projects can be evaluated, permitting organizations to make informed choices. By comparing the payback period of a project with predetermined criteria or industry standards, decision-makers can gauge whether the investment aligns with the organization's goals and expectations. If the payback period surpasses the desired timeframe, it may be necessary to reevaluate the project or seek alternative investment opportunities.

Furthermore, the payback period supports financial planning and forecasting. By assessing the time essential to retrieve the preliminary investment, organizations can incorporate this information into their financial projections. This allows for more accurate cash flow forecasting and budgeting, enabling organizations to make informed decisions about resource allocation and potential financing requirements. It also aids in deciding the project's profitability and overall financial sustainability.

Finally, the payback period can offer perceptions of the project's potential for reinvestment and development. If a project has a short payback period, it designates that the organization can rapidly recover its initial investment and potentially reinvest those funds into new projects or expansion prospects. This endorses a cycle of unceasing growth and development for the organization, enhancing its competitiveness and long-term success.

In a nutshell, the payback period plays a vital part in the project initiation phase by providing valuable information regarding the financial viability, risk assessment, decision-making, financial planning, and growth potential of a project. It serves as a key metric for assessing investment opportunities, helping organizations make informed choices and allocate resources effectively. By comprehending the significance of the payback period, establishments can improve their project selection procedure and enrich their overall financial performance.

5.2.1 Calculation

The payback period is a financial metric used to assess the time it takes for a project to recover its initial investment or generate enough cash flows to cover its costs. It is a straightforward calculation that offers a measure of how rapidly a project can produce positive returns. Mathematically, the payback period can be determined using the following formula:

$$\text{Payback Period} = \frac{\text{Initial Investment}}{\text{Average Annual Cash Inflows}}$$

To apply this formula, you need to consider the following steps:

1. Identify the initial investment: This contains the total cost required to initiate the project, such as equipment, infrastructure, research and development, marketing, and any other applicable expenses.

2. Determine the cash inflows: Compute the anticipated cash inflows for each year of the project's lifetime. These cash inflows represent the net positive cash generated by the project, which can include revenues, cost savings, or any other financial benefits.

3. Calculate the average annual cash inflows: Sum up the cash inflows for each year and divide by the project's lifetime. This will give you the average annual cash inflows.

4. Apply the formula: Divide the initial investment by the average annual cash inflows to calculate the payback period. The result will be expressed in years.

It's significant to note that the payback period calculation does not take into account the time value of money or the profitability of the project beyond the payback period. It emphasizes solely the time essential to recover the initial investment. Therefore, it is a simple metric that provides a rough estimate of the project's financial feasibility and risk.

Moreover, the payback period does not contemplate cash flows beyond the recovery of the initial investment, potentially neglecting the long-term profitability of a project. Therefore, it is often used in combination with other financial metrics, such as Net Present Value (NPV) or Internal Rate of Return (IRR), to offer a more inclusive assessment of a project's financial practicability.

In summary, the payback period calculation technique in the project initiation stage is a comparatively simple mathematical tactic that helps evaluate the time essential to recover the initial investment by dividing it by the average annual cash inflows. However, it should be used in conjunction with other financial metrics for a more detailed analysis of a project's financial possibility.

Example:

Let's say you're considering an investment in a new project that costs $50,000. The project is anticipated to generate annual cash inflows of $15,000 for the next five years.

To compute the payback period, you need to determine how long it will take for the cumulative cash inflows to equal or exceed the preliminary investment.

Step 1: Compute the cumulative cash inflows for each year.
Year 1: $15,000
Year 2: $15,000 + $15,000 = $30,000
Year 3: $30,000 + $15,000 = $45,000
Year 4: $45,000 + $15,000 = $60,000

Step 2: Determine the year when the cumulative cash inflows equal or exceed the initial investment.
The cumulative cash inflows exceed the initial investment of $50,000 in Year 4. So, the accurate payback period would be 3 years and 4 months.

5.2.2 C Code

```c
#include <stdio.h>

float calculatePaybackPeriod(float initialInvestment, float
cashflows[], int numCashflows) {
    float cumulativeCashflow = 0.0;
    int paybackPeriod = 0;

    while (cumulativeCashflow < initialInvestment &&
paybackPeriod < numCashflows) {
        cumulativeCashflow += cashflows[paybackPeriod];
        paybackPeriod++;
    }

    if (cumulativeCashflow < initialInvestment) {
        return -1.0; // Payback period not reached within the
given cash flows
    } else {
        float fractionalPart = (initialInvestment -
(cumulativeCashflow - cashflows[paybackPeriod - 1])) /
cashflows[paybackPeriod - 1];
        return paybackPeriod - 1 + fractionalPart;
    }
}

int main() {
    float initialInvestment;
    int numCashflows;

    printf("Enter the initial investment: ");
    scanf("%f", &initialInvestment);

    printf("Enter the number of cash flows: ");
    scanf("%d", &numCashflows);

    float cashflows[numCashflows];
```

```
printf("Enter the cash flows (separated by spaces):\n");
for (int i = 0; i < numCashflows; i++) {
    scanf("%f", &cashflows[i]);
}

float paybackPeriod =
calculatePaybackPeriod(initialInvestment, cashflows,
numCashflows);
    if (paybackPeriod == -1.0) {
        printf("Payback period not reached within the given
cash flows.\n");
    } else {
        printf("The payback period is %.2f years.\n",
paybackPeriod);
    }

    return 0;
}
```

In this code, the `calculatePaybackPeriod` function takes in the preliminary investment amount, an array of cash flows, and the number of cash flows. It iterates over the cash flows, accumulating them until the cumulative cash flow surpasses the initial investment. It then computes the fractional part of the payback period based on the last cash flow.

In the `main` function, the user is prompted to enter the initial investment, the number of cash flows, and the cash flows themselves. The `calculatePaybackPeriod` function is called with these values, and the result is printed to the console.

5.2.3 JAVA Code

```java
import java.util.Scanner;

public class PaybackPeriodCalculator {
    public static void main(String[] args) {
        Scanner scanner = new Scanner(System.in);

        System.out.print("Enter the initial investment: ");
        double initialInvestment = scanner.nextDouble();

        System.out.print("Enter the number of years: ");
        int years = scanner.nextInt();

        double[] cashFlows = new double[years];

        System.out.println("Enter the cash flows for each year:");
        for (int i = 0; i < years; i++) {
            System.out.print("Year " + (i + 1) + ": ");
            cashFlows[i] = scanner.nextDouble();
        }

        double cumulativeCashFlow = 0;
        int paybackPeriod = 0;

        while (cumulativeCashFlow < initialInvestment &&
paybackPeriod < years) {
            cumulativeCashFlow                            +=
cashFlows[paybackPeriod];
            paybackPeriod++;
        }

        if (paybackPeriod < years) {
            double   fractionalYear   =   (initialInvestment   -
(cumulativeCashFlow - cashFlows[paybackPeriod - 1])) /
cashFlows[paybackPeriod];
```

```
      paybackPeriod += fractionalYear;
    } else {
      paybackPeriod = -1; // Project never recovers the
initial investment
    }

    System.out.println("The payback period is " +
paybackPeriod + " years.");
  }
}
```

In this code, we first prompt the user to enter the initial investment and the number of years for which the cash flows will be considered. Then, we create an array to store the cash flows for each year.

Next, we iterate through the array and ask the user to enter the cash flows for each year. We calculate the cumulative cash flow until it reaches or exceeds the initial investment or until we reach the end of the cash flows array.

If the cumulative cash flow exceeds the initial investment, we calculate the fractional year by subtracting the cumulative cash flow up to the previous year from the initial investment and dividing it by the cash flow for the next year. We add the fractional year to the payback period.

If the payback period is still less than the number of years, we output the payback period. Otherwise, if the payback period exceeds the number of years, it means the project never recovers the initial investment, and we output -1.

Please note that this code assumes the cash flows are provided in consecutive years and does not consider the time value of money.

5.2.4 MATLAB Code

```
% Enter the cash flows for each period
cashFlows = [-1000 200 300 400 500];

% Initialize variables
paybackPeriod = 0;
cumulativeCashFlow = 0;

% Calculate the payback period
for i = 1:length(cashFlows)
    cumulativeCashFlow    =    cumulativeCashFlow    +
cashFlows(i);
    if cumulativeCashFlow >= 0
       paybackPeriod = i;
       break;
    end
end

% Display the result
disp(['The payback period is ' num2str(paybackPeriod) '
years.']);
```

In this example, the cash flows for each period are stored in the `cashFlows` vector. The initial investment is represented as a negative value (-1000), and subsequent cash inflows are positive values (200, 300, 400, 500).

The code then iterates through each cash flow, accumulating the cash flow values in the `cumulativeCashFlow` variable. If the cumulative cash flow becomes positive or zero, indicating that the investment has been recovered, the loop breaks, and the payback period is set to the current iteration index.

Finally, the payback period is displayed using the `disp` function. You can change the `cashFlows` vector to include your cash flow values for different periods.

5.3 Net Present Value

The Net Present Value (NPV) technique is an extensively utilized financial assessment tool for assessing the profitability and viability of investment projects. It is primarily employed in capital budgeting decisions to determine the financial value of future cash flows generated by a project, taking into account the time value of money. The NPV method is considered one of the most reliable techniques for project initiation, as it offers an all-inclusive scrutiny of the potential return on investment.

At its core, the NPV method measures the net value of a project by comparing the present value of all expected cash inflows and outflows associated with the project. It takes into contemplation the fact that the worth of money changes over time due to factors for instance inflation, interest rates, and the cost of capital. By discounting future cash flows to their present value, the NPV method enables decision-makers to determine whether an investment will produce a positive or negative net value.

The calculation of NPV includes three significant steps:
1. Estimating cash flows,
2. Determining the appropriate discount rate, and
3. Discounting cash flows to their present value.

Cash flows characteristically contain initial investment costs, projected revenues, operating expenses, taxes, and salvage value. The discount rate represents the minimum acceptable rate of return and reflects the risk and opportunity cost associated with the investment. It is usually determined by the cost of capital or the company's essential rate of return.

Once the cash flows and discount rate are ascertained, the NPV is computed by subtracting the initial investment from the present value of expected cash inflows. If the NPV is positive, it indicates that the project is expected to generate more value than the initial investment, thus providing a return that exceeds the required rate of return. A positive NPV proposes that the project is economically feasible and should be considered for instigation.

There are numerous benefits to using the NPV technique for project initiation.

Firstly, it considers the time value of money, which recognizes that a dollar received in the future is worth less than a dollar received today. This method allows for a more precise calculation of the project's productivity and helps in comparing investment options with different cash flow patterns.

Secondly, the NPV technique takes into account all pertinent cash flows allied with the venture, including initial investment costs and expected future revenues and expenses. This all-inclusive analysis offers decision-makers a holistic view of the project's financial implications and helps in identifying potential risks and prospects.

Additionally, the NPV technique allows for flexibility in determining the discount rate, which can be adjusted based on the project's risk profile. Projects with higher levels of risk can be assigned a higher discount rate, reflecting the increased opportunity cost of capital. This feature enables decision-makers to make more informed investment decisions and align them with the company's risk appetite. Moreover, the NPV method offers a clear and quantifiable measure of the financial worth of a project, making it easier to communicate and justify investment decisions to stakeholders. It helps in evaluating the impact of the project on the company's general financial performance and enables effective resource provision.

Nevertheless, it is vital to note that the NPV technique has some limitations. One limitation is its reliance on accurate cash flow projections, which can be challenging, especially for long-term projects or those with uncertain revenue streams. The accuracy of the NPV calculation deeply relies on the quality of the assessed cash flows, and any errors or biases in these projections can significantly impact the validity of the results.

Moreover, the NPV method accepts that cash flows are reinvested at the discount rate, which may not always be feasible or realistic. In practice, finding investment opportunities that constantly match the discount rate can be hard, particularly in unstable markets.

In conclusion, the NPV technique is a valued tool for project initiation as it offers a systematic and comprehensive method for assessing the financial feasibility of investment ventures.

5.3.1 Net Present Value Calculation

To compute the net present value (NPV) for project initiation, you need to contemplate the future cash flows associated with the project and discount them to their present value. The NPV aids determine the profitability of the project and whether it is worth pursuing. Here's a step-by-step calculation technique for NPV:

1. Identify the cash flows: Determine the anticipated cash inflows and outflows over the project's lifetime. These can contain preliminary investment costs, operational expenditures, revenues, and salvage values. Cash flows should be assessed for each period, typically annually.

2. Determine the discount rate: The discount rate is the minimum desired rate of return or the cost of capital for the project. It characterizes the opportunity cost of investing in the project rather than pursuing substitute investments with similar risk profiles. The discount rate should reflect the time value of money and integrate the project's risk.

3. Discount cash flows: Apply the discount rate to each cash flow to compute its present value. The present value (PV) of a cash flow is calculated by applying the following formula:

$$PV = \frac{CF}{(1 + r)^n}$$

Where:
- PV is the present value of the cash flow
- CF is the cash flow for a specific period
- r is the discount rate
- n is the number of periods from the present when the cash flow occurs

Repeat this calculation for each cash flow and period.

4. Sum the present values: Add up all the present values of the cash flows calculated in step 3 to determine the total present value (TPV).

5. Compute the NPV: Subtract the initial investment cost (or any initial cash outflows) from the TPV calculated in step 4. The result is the net present value (NPV) of the project.

$$NPV = TPV - \text{Initial Investment}$$

Explanation:

- If NPV > 0: The project is anticipated to generate a positive return and is generally considered financially viable.

- If NPV = 0: The project is anticipated to break even, generating neither profit nor loss.

- If NPV < 0: The project is anticipated to generate a negative return and may not be financially viable.

It's vital to note that NPV analysis is just one factor to consider when assessing a project. Other factors such as risk, strategic alignment, and qualitative considerations should also be taken into account before making a final decision.

Sample Problem:

Company XYZ is considering investing in a project that requires a preliminary investment of $200,000. The project is anticipated to generate cash flows of $50,000 per year for the first three years, and $70,000 per year for the next two years. After that, the project is expected to generate cash flows of $30,000 per year indefinitely. Compute the payback period for this project.

Solution:

To calculate the payback period, we need to determine the time it takes for the cumulative cash flows to equal or exceed the preliminary investment.

Step 1: Calculate the cumulative cash flows for each year.

Year 1: $50,000
Year 2: $50,000 + $50,000 = $100,000
Year 3: $100,000 + $50,000 = $150,000
Year 4: $150,000 + $70,000 = $220,000
Year 5: $220,000 + $70,000 = $290,000
Year 6 onwards: $290,000 + $30,000 = $320,000

Step 2: Determine the year in which the cumulative cash flows exceed the initial investment.

In this case, the cumulative cash flows exceed the initial investment of $200,000 in Year 5.

Step 3: Calculate the fraction of the final year that is needed to recover the remaining investment.

In Year 5, the cumulative cash flow is $290,000. To recover the remaining investment of $200,000, we need an additional $10,000 (since $290,000 - $200,000 = $90,000).

The fraction of the final year needed to recover the remaining investment is $10,000 / $70,000 = 0.143.

Step 4: Compute the payback period.

The payback period is the sum of the years it took to recover the initial investment and the fraction of the final year needed to recover the remaining investment.

Payback period = 5 + 0.143 = 5.143 years.

Therefore, the payback period for this project is approximately 5.143 years.

5.3.2 C Code

```c
#include <stdio.h>
#include <math.h>

double calculateNPV(double cashflows[], double discountRate, int numPeriods) {
    double npv = 0;
    for (int i = 0; i < numPeriods; i++) {
        npv += cashflows[i] / pow(1 + discountRate, i + 1);
    }
    return npv;
}

int main() {
    double cashflows[] = {-1000, 200, 300, 400, 500};
    double discountRate = 0.1;
    int numPeriods = sizeof(cashflows) / sizeof(cashflows[0]);

    double npv = calculateNPV(cashflows, discountRate, numPeriods);

    printf("Net Present Value: %.2f\n", npv);

    return 0;
}
```
```

In this code, we define a function `calculateNPV` that takes an array of cash flows (`cashflows[]`), a discount rate (`discountRate`), and the number of periods (`numPeriods`). It iterates over each cash flow, divides it by the discount factor for the corresponding period, and accumulates the results in the `npv` variable.

In the `main` function, we initialize the `cashflows[]` array
```

with the cash flow values (-1000, 200, 300, 400, 500), set the `discountRate` to 0.1 (10%), and calculate the `numPeriods` based on the array size. We then call the `calculateNPV` function with these values and store the result in the `npv` variable. Finally, we print the NPV to the console.

Note that this code assumes the cash flows are already adjusted for the time value of money (i.e., discounted cash flows). If the cash flows are not discounted, you may need to adjust the code accordingly by multiplying each cash flow by the appropriate discount factor.

5.3.3 JAVA Code

```java
import java.util.Scanner;

public class NetPresentValueCalculator {
    public static void main(String[] args) {
        Scanner scanner = new Scanner(System.in);

        System.out.print("Enter the discount rate: ");
        double discountRate = scanner.nextDouble();

        System.out.print("Enter the number of periods: ");
        int periods = scanner.nextInt();

        double[] cashFlows = new double[periods];
        for (int i = 0; i < periods; i++) {
            System.out.print("Enter the cash flow for period "
+ (i + 1) + ": ");
            cashFlows[i] = scanner.nextDouble();
        }
        double    npv    =    calculateNPV(cashFlows,
discountRate);
        System.out.println("The net present value is: " + npv);

        scanner.close();
    }

    public static double calculateNPV(double[] cashFlows,
double discountRate) {
        double npv = 0.0;
        for (int i = 0; i < cashFlows.length; i++) {
            npv += cashFlows[i] / Math.pow(1 + discountRate,
i + 1);
        }
        return npv;
    }
}
```

In this code, we first prompt the user to enter the discount rate and the number of periods. Then, we create an array `cashFlows` to store the cash flows for each period, and we ask the user to input the cash flow for each period.

Next, we call the `calculateNPV` method, which takes the `cashFlows` array and the `discountRate` as arguments. Inside this method, we iterate over each cash flow and calculate the present value using the formula `cashFlow / (1 + discountRate)^period`. We sum up all the present values to get the net present value.

Finally, we print the calculated NPV to the console. Please note that this code assumes the cash flows are provided in the accurate order and that the user enters valid numerical inputs.

5.3.4 Python Code

```python
def      calculate_npv(initial_investment,      cash_flows,
discount_rate):
    npv = -initial_investment
    for i, cash_flow in enumerate(cash_flows):
        npv += cash_flow / ((1 + discount_rate) ** (i + 1))
    return npv

# Example usage
initial_investment = 10000
cash_flows = [2000, 3000, 4000, 5000, 6000]
discount_rate = 0.1

npv   =   calculate_npv(initial_investment,   cash_flows,
discount_rate)
print("Net Present Value (NPV):", npv)
```

In the above code, the `calculate_npv` function takes three arguments: `initial_investment`, `cash_flows`, and `discount_rate`. The `initial_investment` represents the initial investment or cost of the project. `cash_flows` is a list of cash flows generated by the project over a specific time, and `discount_rate` is the rate at which future cash flows are discounted to their present value.

The function computes the NPV by subtracting the initial investment from the sum of the present values of each cash flow. The present value is calculated by dividing each cash flow by `(1 + discount_rate) ** (i + 1)`, where `i` is the index of the cash flow in the `cash_flows` list.

In the example usage, we provide a sample `initial_investment` of $10,000, `cash_flows` of [2000, 3000, 4000, 5000, 6000] (representing cash flows over five periods), and a `discount_rate` of 0.1 (or 10%). The calculated NPV is then printed to the console. Feel free to change the inputs to match your precise project particulars.

5.3.5 MATLAB Code

```
% Project Cash Flows
cashFlows = [-1000 300 300 300 300 300];

% Discount Rate
discountRate = 0.1;

% Calculate Net Present Value (NPV)
npv                                    =
sum(cashFlows./(1+discountRate).^(0:length(cashFlows)-
1));

% Display the Net Present Value
fprintf('The Net Present Value (NPV) for the project
initiation is: $%.2f\n', npv);
```

In this example, we assume that the project has an initial investment of $1000 (negative value) and generates cash inflows of $300 at the end of each period for 5 periods. The discount rate is set to 0.1 (10%). The code calculates the NPV by discounting each cash flow to its present value and summing them up.

You can modify the `cashFlows` and `discountRate` variables to match your project's specific cash flow values and discount rate. The NPV will be displayed in the console output.

Note: This code accepts that the cash flows are evenly spaced and happen after each period. If your cash flows have dissimilar timing, you will need to fine-tune the code consequently.

5.4 Return on Investment

The return on investment (ROI) technique is a critical tool employed during the project initiation stage to evaluate the possible benefits and worth of a project. It provides stakeholders with a quantitative analysis of the expected return compared to the investment required, permitting them to make knowledgeable decisions about project viability and prioritize resource allocation.

Throughout the project initiation stage, organizations assess various project proposals to determine which ones align with their strategic objectives and offer the greatest return on investment. The ROI technique helps in this evaluation process by calculating the financial gains and benefits expected from a project relative to the costs incurred.

To implement the ROI scheme, project administrators and stakeholders recognize and quantify both the costs and benefits associated with the project. Costs include direct expenses such as labor, equipment, and materials, as well as indirect costs like overhead and administrative expenses. Benefits, on the other hand, may contain increased revenue, cost savings, improved customer satisfaction, or improved operational competence.

Once the costs and benefits are recognized, the ROI is calculated using the following formula:

$$ROI = \frac{\text{Net Benefit}}{\text{Cost}} \times 100$$

The net benefit is determined by subtracting the total costs from the total benefits. A positive ROI specifies that the project is anticipated to produce more worth than it costs, making it an attractive investment prospect.

The ROI technique offers numerous advantages in the project initiation stage. Firstly, it helps in comparing and prioritizing projects based on their probable returns. By quantifying the financial impact, organizations can allocate their limited resources to the projects that offer the highest ROI, guaranteeing optimal utilization and minimizing the risk of investing in projects with low returns.

Secondly, the ROI method facilitates decision-making by providing stakeholders with a clear and objective measure of project feasibility. It permits them to make informed choices about whether to proceed with a project, seek additional funding, or explore alternative options.

Additionally, the ROI technique assists in setting realistic project goals and objectives. By scrutinizing the probable benefits and costs, organizations can create attainable targets, identify potential risks, and develop contingency strategies.

Nevertheless, it is imperative to note that the ROI method has its limitations. It mainly focuses on financial returns and may not capture other qualitative or strategic factors. For instance, a project with a lower ROI may still be valuable if it aligns with long-term strategic goals or contributes to intangible benefits like brand reputation or employee morale. Consequently, establishments must consider an all-inclusive assessment that incorporates both quantitative and qualitative factors in their project evaluation procedure.

To put it briefly, the ROI technique plays a vital role in the project initiation stage by providing a quantitative analysis of the expected return on investment. By considering the costs and benefits of a project, organizations can make informed decisions, prioritize resources, and establish realistic project goals. Although the ROI technique is a valuable tool, it should be used in combination with other assessment techniques to guarantee a complete assessment of project viability and potential value.

5.4.1 Algorithm

Certainly! Here's a simplified algorithm for calculating the return on investment (ROI):

1. Start by gathering the necessary information:
   - Initial investment amount (I)
   - Final investment value (F)
   - Time (T)

2. Calculate the ROI using the following formula:
   - ROI = ((F - I) / I) * 100

3. Return the calculated ROI.

Here's a Python implementation of the algorithm:

```python
def     calculate_roi(initial_investment,      final_value,
time_period):
    roi   =   ((final_value   -   initial_investment)   /
initial_investment) * 100
    return roi

# Example usage:
initial_investment = 10000
final_value = 12000
time_period = 2

roi   =    calculate_roi(initial_investment,      final_value,
time_period)
print("ROI: {:.2f}%".format(roi))
```

In this example, an initial investment of $10,000 has grown to $12,000 over 2 years. The calculated ROI is 20%.

5.5 Project Charter

A project charter is a formal record that offers a summary of a project's purposes, scope, deliverables, stakeholders, and crucial milestones. It serves as a reference point and foundation for the project, establishing its purpose, goals, and the authority of the project manager to execute it. Here are some key elements typically included in a project charter:

1. Project Title and Description: The charter starts with a concise and descriptive title for the project, followed by a summary outlining the purpose, objectives, and expected outcomes.

2. Project Scope: This section describes the boundaries of the project, including what is included and excluded. It clarifies the project's focus and helps manage expectations.

3. Objectives and Deliverables: The project charter summarizes the specific goals and desired consequences of the project. It identifies the deliverables that will be produced and the criteria for measuring their success.

4. Stakeholders: The charter identifies the key individuals or groups who have an interest in the project, including the project sponsor, stakeholders, and project team members. It defines their roles and responsibilities and establishes lines of communication.

5. Project Timeline: A project charter normally comprises a high-level timeline or schedule indicating major milestones and deadlines. This helps in setting expectations and provides a reference for project progress tracking.

6. Assumptions and Constraints: Assumptions are factors or conditions that are believed to be true but are not yet verified, while constraints are limitations or restrictions that affect the project. Identifying these factors upfront helps manage risks and expectations.

7. Budget and Resources: The project charter may include a preliminary budget estimate and resource requirements, such as personnel, equipment, and materials. This information assists in resource planning and allocation.

8. Risks and Dependencies: This section emphasizes potential risks and dependencies that may impact the project's success. It encourages early identification and mitigation of risks and helps in anticipating and managing interdependencies with other projects or stakeholders.

9. Approval and Signatures: The project charter ends with the necessary approval and sign-off from pertinent stakeholders, representing their support and commitment to the project.

The project charter serves as a guiding document through the project lifecycle, providing a shared understanding of the project's purposes and boundaries. It aids stakeholders align their efforts, enables effective communication, and facilitates decision-making. The charter is typically created during the initiation stage of a project and may be updated as required throughout its implementation.

5.5.1 Sample Project Charter

[Project Name]

Project Charter

[Project Name]: [Insert Project Name]
Project Manager: [Insert Project Manager Name]
Date: [Insert Date]

1. Project Overview

The purpose of this document is to establish a clear understanding of the objectives, scope, deliverables, stakeholders, and key success factors of the [Project Name]. This project charter outlines the initial framework and provides a solid foundation for effective project management and decision-making throughout the project lifecycle.

2. Project Objectives

The primary objectives of the [Project Name] are as follows:

- [Insert Objective 1]
- [Insert Objective 2]
- [Insert Objective 3]
- [Insert Objective 4]
- [Insert Objective 5]

These objectives align with the strategic goals and priorities of the organization and aim to deliver specific outcomes that meet the needs of the project stakeholders.

3. Project Scope

The scope of the [Project Name] includes:

- [Insert Scope 1]
- [Insert Scope 2]
- [Insert Scope 3]
- [Insert Scope 4]
- [Insert Scope 5]

The project scope defines the boundaries and deliverables of the project, outlining what will be included and excluded from the project work.

4. Project Deliverables

The key deliverables of the [Project Name] are:

- [Insert Deliverable 1]
- [Insert Deliverable 2]
- [Insert Deliverable 3]
- [Insert Deliverable 4]
- [Insert Deliverable 5]

These deliverables represent tangible outputs that will be produced throughout the project, contributing to the achievement of the project objectives.

5. Project Stakeholders

The primary stakeholders involved in the [Project Name] include:

- [Insert Stakeholder 1]
- [Insert Stakeholder 2]
- [Insert Stakeholder 3]
- [Insert Stakeholder 4]
- [Insert Stakeholder 5]

It is important to identify and engage these stakeholders

effectively, ensuring their needs, expectations, and concerns are addressed throughout the project.

6. Key Success Factors

The success of the [Project Name] will be determined by the following factors:

- [Insert Success Factor 1]
- [Insert Success Factor 2]
- [Insert Success Factor 3]
- [Insert Success Factor 4]
- [Insert Success Factor 5]

These factors will be monitored and measured to assess the progress and overall success of the project.

7. Project Constraints

The [Project Name] will operate within the following constraints:

- [Insert Constraint 1]
- [Insert Constraint 2]
- [Insert Constraint 3]
- [Insert Constraint 4]
- [Insert Constraint 5]

These constraints may include budget limitations, resource availability, time constraints, or any other factors that may impact the project's execution.

8. Project Assumptions

The [Project Name] is based on the following assumptions:

- [Insert Assumption 1]

- [Insert Assumption 2]
- [Insert Assumption 3]
- [Insert Assumption 4]
- [Insert Assumption 5]

These assumptions provide a basis for planning and decision-making throughout the project but should be periodically reviewed and validated.

9. Project Risks

The [Project Name] is subject to the following risks:

- [Insert Risk 1]
- [Insert Risk 2]
- [Insert Risk 3]
- [Insert Risk 4]
- [Insert Risk 5]

A comprehensive risk management plan will be developed and implemented to identify, assess, and mitigate these risks effectively.

10. Project Governance

The [Project Name] will be governed by a project steering committee consisting of the following members:

- [Insert Committee Member 1]
- [Insert Committee Member 2]
- [Insert Committee

 Member 3]
- [Insert Committee Member 4]
- [Insert Committee Member 5]

The project steering committee will provide guidance,

oversight, and decision-making authority throughout the project lifecycle.

11. Project Timeline

The estimated timeline for the [Project Name] is as follows:

- [Insert Milestone 1]
- [Insert Milestone 2]
- [Insert Milestone 3]
- [Insert Milestone 4]
- [Insert Milestone 5]

This timeline represents a preliminary schedule and may be subject to adjustments based on project needs and constraints.

12. Approval

This project charter is approved and accepted by:

[Insert Name]
[Insert Title]
[Insert Date]

[Insert Name]
[Insert Title]
[Insert Date]

[Insert Name]
[Insert Title]
[Insert Date]

[Insert Name]
[Insert Title]
[Insert Date]

[Insert Name]
[Insert Title]
[Insert Date]

By signing this document, the project team and stakeholders acknowledge their commitment to the objectives, scope, and success factors outlined in the project charter.

_____   _____

[Project Manager]   [Date]

_____   _____

[Project Sponsor]   [Date]

_____   _____

[Steering Committee Member 1]   [Date]

_____   _____

[Steering Committee Member 2]   [Date]

_____   _____

[Steering Committee Member 3]   [Date]

Note: This project charter serves as a high-level document and will be further detailed and refined in subsequent project management documents such as the project plan, risk register, and communication plan.

5.6 Exercise

1. What is the purpose of the project initiation phase?

2. Who are the key stakeholders that should be involved in the project initiation phase?

3. What are the main objectives and deliverables of the project initiation phase?

4. How do you define the scope of the project during the initiation phase?

5. What are the key risks and assumptions to be identified and documented in the initiation phase?

6. What is the process for selecting the project team members during the initiation phase?

7. What are the key constraints and dependencies that need to be considered in the initiation phase?

8. What are the high-level project requirements that should be defined during the initiation phase?

9. How do you determine the project's timeline and milestones in the initiation phase?

10. What are the key success criteria for the project, and how do you establish them during the initiation phase?

11. What are the key communication channels and stakeholders' roles in the initiation phase?

12. How do you conduct a feasibility study and assess the project's viability during the initiation phase?

13. What are the different project management methodologies or frameworks that can be considered

during the initiation phase?

14. How do you identify and prioritize the project's key objectives and goals in the initiation phase?

15. What are the key assumptions and constraints related to the project's budget and resources during the initiation phase?

16. How do you identify and document the project's organizational structure and reporting lines during the initiation phase?

17. What are the key project documentation and templates that need to be created or reviewed during the initiation phase?

18. How do you conduct a stakeholder analysis and identify the project's key influencers and decision-makers during the initiation phase?

19. What are the legal and regulatory requirements that need to be considered and complied with in the initiation phase?

20. How do you identify and assess the project's potential risks and develop a risk management plan during the initiation phase?

21. What are the key procurement requirements and considerations that need to be addressed in the initiation phase?

22. How do you define and prioritize the project's objectives and goals in alignment with the organization's strategic priorities during the initiation phase?

23. What are the key performance indicators (KPIs) that should be established to measure the project's success during the initiation phase?

24. How do you conduct a stakeholder needs analysis and identify the project's key requirements and expectations during the initiation phase?

25. What are the different project deliverables and their dependencies that need to be identified and defined during the initiation phase?

26. How do you establish the project's governance structure and decision-making processes during the initiation phase?

27. What are the key lessons learned from previous similar projects that should be considered in the initiation phase?

28. How do you identify and assess the project's resource requirements, including personnel, equipment, and facilities, during the initiation phase?

29. What are the different project constraints, such as time, cost, quality, and scope, and how do you prioritize them during the initiation phase?

30. How do you develop and obtain approval for the project charter or project initiation document during the initiation phase?

6 Scope Planning

6.1 Important Activities

Project management is an organized approach to planning, executing, and controlling projects to achieve specific goals and objectives within defined constraints. The achievement of any project depends on how well it is planned and managed, and the scope planning phase is a critical part of the project management process. The scope planning stage involves defining and documenting the project's objectives, deliverables, and boundaries, as well as identifying the work required to accomplish those objectives. In this section, we will delve into the particulars of the scope planning stage in project management.

The scope planning stage is the first step in the general project management procedure. It sets the groundwork for the project by defining its limitations and clarifying what is included and what is not. This phase is vital as it helps stakeholders and project team associates gain a shared understanding of the project's purpose, goals, and objectives.

The important events in the scope planning stage comprise:

1. Project Commencement: This includes defining the project's purpose, identifying the stakeholders, and establishing the project's objectives. It is significant to include key stakeholders from the start to guarantee their buy-in and support throughout the project.

2. Scope Statement: The scope statement is a detailed document that defines the project's deliverables, boundaries, and objectives. It describes what is included and what is excluded from the project. The scope statement provides a clear understanding of the project's purpose and helps manage expectations.

3. Work Breakdown Structure (WBS): The WBS is a hierarchical decomposition of the project's deliverables into smaller, more manageable work packages. It breaks down the project into smaller components, making it easier to estimate and manage the work required. The WBS serves as a foundation for project scheduling, cost estimation, and resource allocation.

4. Scope Verification: Scope verification ensures that all the project deliverables have been completed satisfactorily and meet the defined requirements. It involves obtaining formal acceptance from the stakeholders that the project's deliverables are complete and meet their opportunities. Scope verification supports prevent scope creep and warrants that the project stays within its defined boundaries.

5. Scope Change Control: Scope change control is a procedure to manage and control changes to the project's opportunity. It includes evaluating proposed changes, determining their impact on the project's objectives, and making informed decisions about whether to approve or reject them. Scope change control helps maintain project focus and prevents uncontrolled scope changes that can lead to project delays, budget overruns, and customer dissatisfaction.

The scope planning stage requires effective communication and teamwork among stakeholders and project team members. It is important to engage stakeholders and solicit their input to guarantee that the project's objectives and boundaries are clearly defined. Consistent communication and collaboration help build consensus and alignment among the project team and stakeholders, leading to a shared understanding of the project's scope.

One of the significant outputs of the scope planning stage is the Project Scope Statement. The Project Scope Statement is a comprehensive document that describes the project's objectives, deliverables, constraints, and assumptions. It provides a clear definition of the project's scope and acts as a reference point throughout the project lifecycle. The Project Scope Statement helps project managers and team members make decisions regarding the project's scope, and it also serves as a communication tool to manage stakeholders' expectations.

Another important output of the scope planning phase is the Work Breakdown Structure (WBS). The WBS breaks down the project's deliverables into smaller, controllable work packages. It provides a hierarchical structure that helps in organizing and understanding the project's components. The WBS serves as the foundation for developing project schedules, assessing costs, and assigning resources. It also helps in identifying dependencies between different work packages and facilitates effective project tracking and control.

Throughout the scope planning phase, it is vital to identify and manage risks associated with the project's scope. Risks can arise from incomplete or ambiguous scope definitions, changing requirements, or external features beyond the project team's control. It is important to conduct a thorough risk analysis and develop appropriate risk mitigation strategies to address potential risks to the project's scope. Regular monitoring and review of the project's scope throughout the project lifecycle help in identifying and addressing scope-related risks proactively.

Effective scope planning also includes considering the project's constraints, such as time, cost, and resources. It is important to balance these constrictions and guarantee that the project's scope is achievable within the given constraints. Scope planning helps in setting realistic expectations and managing stakeholders' and team members' expectations regarding the project's scope, schedule, and budget.

The scope planning stage is closely linked to other project management processes, such as time management, cost management, and risk management. The scope defines the boundaries of the project and influences the project's schedule, budget, and resource apportionment. Changes to the project's scope can impact the project's schedule, cost, and overall success. Therefore, effective scope planning and control are essential for project success.

To sum up, the scope planning phase is a critical component of project management. It involves defining and documenting the project's purposes, deliverables, and boundaries. The scope planning phase sets the foundation for the project, helps manage stakeholders' expectations, and facilitates effective project execution and control. By clearly defining the project's scope, developing a comprehensive scope statement, and creating a detailed work breakdown structure, project administrators and team associates can efficiently plan and manage the project's scope, schedule, and budget.

6.2 Functional Requirements

In project scope planning, both functional and non-functional requirements play vital roles. Let's compare them:

1. Description: Functional requirements specify what the system or product should do and how it should behave to meet the users' needs. They describe the system's features, capabilities, and interactions with users and other systems.

2. Emphasis: Functional requirements are concerned with the system's functionality and the desired outcomes it should achieve.

3. Instances: Functional requirements can include specific actions, tasks, calculations, data processing, user interfaces, and any other expected behavior of the system. For example, "The system should allow users to create, edit, and delete customer records" or "The system should generate a monthly sales report."

4. Testability: Functional requirements can be tested to determine whether the system meets the specified criteria or not. They provide clear guidelines for testing and validation.

6.3 Non-functional Requirements

1. Description: Non-functional requirements specify the quality attributes and constrictions that the system must adhere to. They focus on characteristics such as performance, reliability, security, usability, scalability, and maintainability.

2. Emphasis: Non-functional requirements are concerned with how the system should perform and its overall behavior, rather than specific features or functions.

3. Instances: Non-functional requirements can include response time, system availability, security procedures, user experience, maintainability standards, and performance benchmarks. For example, "The system should respond to user input within 2 seconds" or "The system should be available 99.9% of the time."

4. Evaluation: Non-functional requirements are often evaluated through testing, benchmarking, and performance monitoring. They are evaluated based on predefined criteria and industry standards.

6.4 Key Differences

1. Purpose: Functional requirements focus on defining specific system functions and user interactions, while non-functional requirements emphasize the system's overall qualities and constraints.

2. Content: Functional requirements specify what the system should do, while non-functional requirements define how the system should perform.

3. Testability vs. Evaluation: Functional requirements can be easily tested for compliance, whereas non-functional requirements often require evaluation through performance monitoring, benchmarking, and subjective assessments.

4. User Focus: Functional requirements address user needs and desired system behavior, while non-functional requirements ensure that the system meets performance, security, and usability expectations.

In summary, functional requirements define what the system should do, focusing on specific features and tasks, while non-functional requirements specify the system's overall behavior and quality attributes, such as performance, reliability, and usability. Both kinds of requirements are essential for effective project scope planning and confirming a successful system implementation.

6.5 Requirement Traceability Matrix

A requirement traceability matrix (RTM) is a tool used in project management and software development to guarantee that all requirements are met and properly executed throughout the project lifespan. It establishes a clear link between various project artifacts, such as requirements, design documents, test cases, and deliverables.

The main purpose of an RTM is to track and verify the alignment between diverse project stages, making it easier to recognize any gaps or inconsistencies. Mapping requirements to other project elements, enables effective change management, impact analysis, and quality assurance.

Here's an example to demonstrate the concept of a requirement traceability matrix:

Assume we are developing a web-based e-commerce platform, and we have the succeeding requirements:

1. Requirement: User registration
   - Design: User registration form
   - Development: User registration functionality
   - Testing: Verify successful user registration

2. Requirement: Product catalog
   - Design: Database schema for products
   - Development: Backend API for fetching product data

   - Testing: Validate product information retrieval

3. Requirement: Shopping cart
   - Design: Shopping cart UI wireframes
   - Development: Implement shopping cart functionality
   - Testing: Verify adding/removing items from the cart

4. Requirement: Payment gateway integration
   - Design: Integration architecture with payment provider
   - Development: Implement payment gateway API calls
   - Testing: Validate successful payment transactions

In the requirement traceability matrix, we can create a table with requirements on the leftmost column and project artifacts as headers of the subsequent columns. The matrix may look like this:

Requirement	Design	Development	Testing
User registration	Form	Function	Verify
Product catalog	Schema	API	Validate
Shopping cart	UI wireframes	Function	Verify
Payment gateway integration	Integration architecture	API	Validate

Utilizing this matrix, we can easily identify which design components, development tasks, and testing activities are associated with each requirement. It helps project stakeholders track the progress and ensures that all requirements have been addressed and tested suitably.

In conclusion, a requirement traceability matrix is a valuable tool that promotes transparency, reliability, and wholeness in project management. It aids in maintaining a clear understanding of the relations between requirements and various project artifacts, enabling effective project planning, tracking, and quality assurance.

6.6 Work Breakdown Structure

The Work Breakdown Structure (WBS) is a hierarchical decomposition of a project into smaller, more controllable components. Mathematically, we can characterize the WBS as a tree structure. Let's break it down step by step:

1. Root Node: The root node characterizes the entire project. It is the highest level of the WBS hierarchy and encompasses all the project's deliverables and objectives. We can denote it as R.

2. Levels: The WBS consists of several levels, each representing a diverse level of detail and decomposition. The number of levels can vary depending on the complexity of the project. Let's denote the levels as L1, L2, L3, and so on, with L1 being the highest level below the root node.

3. Nodes: Each level in the WBS consists of multiple nodes, representing the work packages or deliverables. We can denote the nodes as N11, N12, N21, N22, N23, and so on, where the first digit represents the level and the second digit represents the position of the node within that level.

4. Relationships: The WBS also includes relationships between the nodes. The relationship between a parent node and its child nodes represents the hierarchical structure. For example, a node at level L1 can have child nodes at level L2, and a node at level L2 can have child nodes at level L3, and so on.

5. Decomposition: The WBS is created through a process of decomposition, where each node is further broken down into smaller, more manageable sub-packages. This process continues until the work packages are at a level that can be easily assigned, estimated, and managed.

6. Leaf Nodes: The leaf nodes of the WBS represent the smallest components of work that cannot be further decomposed. These are the final deliverables or activities that need to be completed. We can denote the leaf nodes as LN111, LN112, LN121, LN122, LN123, and so on, where the first two digits represent the level, and the third digit represents the position of the node within that level.

7. Work Packages: Each node in the WBS represents a work package, which is a set of related activities or deliverables. Work packages are the building blocks of the project, and they can be assigned to specific individuals or teams for execution.

By forming the project into a hierarchical structure, the WBS provides a visual representation of the project scope, the relationship between the different components, and a clear breakdown of the work essential to complete the project. This helps in estimating the project's cost, duration, and resource requirements, as well as in tracking development and handling project risks.

Here's an example of WBS for a software development project:

Project: Develop a Mobile Application

1. Project Initiation
    1.1 Define project scope and objectives
    1.2 Identify project stakeholders
    1.3 Create a project charter

2. Requirements Gathering
    2.1 Conduct user interviews
    2.2 Document functional requirements
    2.3 Identify technical requirements
    2.4 Define user stories and acceptance criteria

3. Design Phase
    3.1 Create wireframes and prototypes
    3.2 Design user interface (UI) and user experience (UX)
    3.3 Develop database schema
    3.4 Define system architecture

4. Development Phase
    4.1 Set up a development environment
    4.2 Implement backend functionality
        4.2.1 User authentication
        4.2.2 Data storage and retrieval
        4.2.3 API integration
    4.3 Implement frontend components

4.3.1 User interface design
4.3.2 User interactions and navigation
4.3.3 Error handling and validation
4.4 Perform unit testing

5. Testing and Quality Assurance
   5.1 Develop test cases and scenarios
   5.2 Perform functional testing
   5.3 Conduct usability testing
   5.4 Perform performance testing
   5.5 Address and resolve defects

6. Deployment
   6.1 Prepare deployment environment
   6.2 Deploy the application to app stores
   6.3 Configure server and database infrastructure
   6.4 Perform final testing in the production environment

7. User Acceptance Testing (UAT)
   7.1 Coordinate UAT with stakeholders
   7.2 Collect feedback and incorporate necessary changes

8. Training and Documentation
   8.1 Develop user manuals and documentation
   8.2 Conduct training sessions for users

9. Project Closure
   9.1 Obtain sign-off from stakeholders
   9.2 Document lessons learned
   9.3 Archive project documentation and deliverables

Note that this is just a simplified instance and the real WBS for a project can be more exhaustive and tailored based on the precise necessities and opportunities of the project.

6.7 Exercise

1. What is the purpose of scope planning in the project initiation phase?
2. What are the key objectives of scope planning?
3. Who should be involved in the scope planning process?
4. How does scope planning contribute to project success?
5. What are the main deliverables of the scope planning process?
6. How do you define project scope?
7. What techniques can be used to gather requirements for scope planning?
8. How do you prioritize project requirements during scope planning?
9. What factors should be considered when determining the project's boundaries and limitations?
10. How do you handle changes to the project scope during the initiation phase?
11. What documentation should be produced during scope planning?
12. How do you ensure that all stakeholders' expectations are considered during scope planning?
13. What tools or software can assist with scope planning?
14. How do you identify and manage risks related to project scope?
15. What strategies can be employed to ensure the project

scope is realistic and achievable?

16. How do you determine the project's timeline and milestones during scope planning?

17. What techniques can be used to estimate the resources required for the project scope?

18. How do you define the project's success criteria during scope planning?

19. What considerations should be taken into account when defining project constraints?

20. How do you ensure that the project scope aligns with the organization's strategic goals?

21. What methods can be used to communicate the project scope to stakeholders?

22. How do you handle conflicts or disagreements regarding project scope during the initiation phase?

23. What techniques can be used to ensure that the project scope is well understood by the project team?

24. How do you identify dependencies and interdependencies within the project scope?

25. What strategies can be used to mitigate scope creep during the initiation phase?

26. How do you ensure that the project scope is feasible within the given budget?

27. What considerations should be made when defining the project's assumptions and constraints?

28. How do you document and track changes to the project scope throughout the initiation phase?

29. What processes should be followed to gain approval for the project scope?

30. How do you ensure that the project scope remains aligned with the project's objectives and goals throughout its lifecycle?

7 Project Schedule Planning

7.1 Steps for Project Scheduling

Project schedule planning is a crucial aspect of project management that involves defining and organizing the activities required to complete a project within a specified timeframe. It serves as a roadmap for the project, outlining the sequence, duration, and dependencies of tasks, as well as the project's overall timeline.

The process of project schedule planning typically begins with identifying the project's objectives, deliverables, and requirements. This information forms the basis for creating a work breakdown structure (WBS), which breaks down the project into smaller, manageable tasks. Each task is then assigned a duration estimate and dependencies are determined, taking into account any relationships or constraints between tasks.

Once the responsibilities and dependencies are recognized, the project manager can create a project schedule. This involves determining the start and end dates for each task, considering factors such as resource availability, critical path analysis, and any constraints or limitations imposed by the project or organization.

There are numerous techniques and tools available to aid in project schedule planning, such as Gantt charts, network diagrams, and project management software. These tools help visualize the project schedule, highlight critical tasks, and facilitate communication and coordination among team members.

Consistent monitoring and control of the project schedule are essential to ensure that the project stays on track. The project manager should regularly review and update the schedule, taking into account any changes, delays, or unforeseen circumstances that may arise during the project's execution. Adjustments may be required to maintain the project's timeline and meet its objectives.

Effective project schedule planning helps improve project efficiency, manage resources effectively, and mitigate risks associated with time constraints. It enables stakeholders to have a clear understanding of the project's progress, milestones, and deadlines. By setting realistic timelines and allocating resources suitably, project schedule planning contributes to the successful completion of projects within the desired timeframes.

Project schedule planning involves creating a roadmap that outlines the tasks, activities, milestones, and resources required to complete a project within a specified timeframe. Here are some steps to help you with project schedule planning:

Step 1: Define the project scope and objectives.
- Clearly understand and document the goals, deliverables, and requirements of the project.
- Identify any constraints, such as budget limitations or resource availability.

Step 2: Break down the project into tasks.
- Decompose the project into smaller, manageable tasks.
- Ensure that each task is specific, measurable, achievable, relevant, and time-bound (SMART).

Step 3: Determine task dependencies.
- Identify the relationships between tasks.
- Determine which tasks can start only after certain other tasks are completed (predecessors).

Step 4: Estimate task durations.
- Estimate the amount of time needed to complete each task.
- Consider factors like complexity, resources required, and historical data.

Step 5: Determine resource requirements.
- Identify the types and quantities of resources needed for each task.
- Consider human resources, equipment, materials, and any external dependencies.

Step 6: Create a project schedule.
- Use project management software or tools to create a visual representation of the schedule.
- Arrange the tasks in chronological order, considering their dependencies and durations.
- Allocate resources to each task based on availability and requirements.

Step 7: Optimize the schedule.
- Review the project schedule to identify any potential bottlenecks or resource conflicts.
- Adjust task durations or resource assignments if necessary to optimize the schedule.
- Ensure that the project can be completed within the allocated time frame.

Step 8: Set milestones.
- Define key milestones or checkpoints within the project schedule.
- Milestones help track progress and provide a sense of achievement throughout the project.

Step 9: Communicate the schedule.
- Share the project schedule with all relevant stakeholders.
- Ensure that everyone understands their roles, responsibilities, and deadlines.

Step 10: Monitor and update the schedule.
- Regularly track the progress of tasks and update the schedule accordingly.
- Identify any deviations from the planned schedule and take corrective actions as needed.
- Communicate any changes to the stakeholders and adjust the schedule as required.

Remember, project scheduling is an iterative procedure, and alterations may be compulsory as the project progresses.

7.2 Gannt Chart

A Gantt chart is a visual tool used in project management to plan, schedule, and track progress over time. It provides a clear and comprehensive representation of project tasks, their durations, dependencies, and deadlines. The chart consists of horizontal bars representing individual tasks or activities, plotted along a timeline.

Let's consider an example of a project to understand how a Gantt chart can be used effectively.

Tasks

This column should be ordered sequentially.	*Enter the start date for each task below. For best results sort this column in ascending order.*	*Enter the end date for each task or activity below, in this column.*	*Enter tasks and/or activities in this column.*
No.	**Start Date**	**End Date**	**Task**
1	31-05-2023	01-06-2023	Activity 1
2	01-06-2023	02-06-2023	Activity 2
3	01-06-2023	06-06-2023	Activity 3
4	02-06-2023	09-06-2023	Activity 4
5	09-06-2023	19-06-2023	Activity 5
6	13-06-2023	13-07-2023	Activity 6
7	16-06-2023	01-07-2023	Activity 7
8	26-06-2023	01-07-2023	Activity 8
9	05-07-2023	07-07-2023	Activity 9
10	11-07-2023	10-08-2023	Activity 10
11	13-07-2023	05-08-2023	Activity 11
12	21-07-2023	26-07-2023	Activity 12

PROJECT MANAGEMENT

Milestones

This column should be ordered sequentially.	*The position column, charts milestones within the task chart.*	*Enter the date for a milestone in this column.*	*Enter a milestone description in this column. These descriptions will appear in the chart.*
No.	**Position**	**Date**	**Milestone**
1	1	10-06-2023	Milestone 1
2	1	26-06-2023	Milestone 2
3	1	06-07-2023	Milestone 3
4	1	16-07-2023	Milestone 4
5	1	31-07-2023	Milestone 5
6	1	10-08-2023	Milestone 6

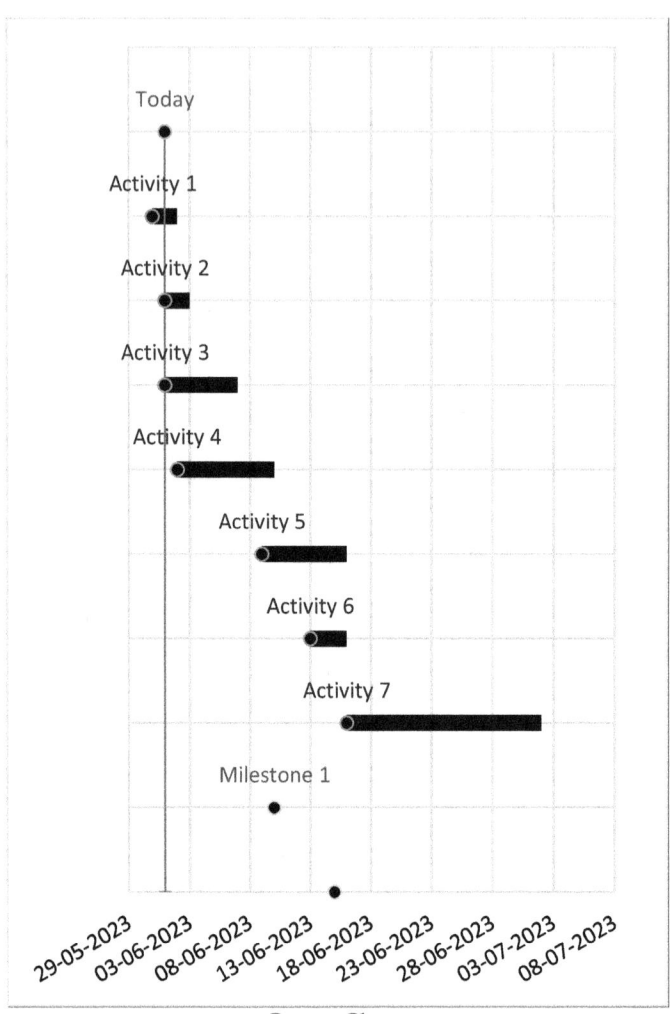

Gannt Chart

By visually representing the project tasks and their durations, the Gantt chart allows project managers to identify potential bottlenecks, dependencies, and critical paths. It helps in coordinating activities, allocating resources, and tracking progress throughout the project lifecycle.

Project team members can refer to the Gantt chart to understand their responsibilities, deadlines, and how their tasks align with the overall project timeline. It serves as a communication tool, ensuring that everyone involved in the project has a shared understanding of the project's progress and milestones.

Gantt charts are dynamic and can be updated as the project progresses. As tasks are completed or delayed, the chart can be adjusted to reflect the changes, enabling project managers to adapt their plans and make informed decisions.

In summary, a Gantt chart provides a visual representation of project tasks, durations, and dependencies, helping project managers and teams effectively plan, schedule, and track progress throughout the project lifecycle.

7.3 Network Diagram and Critical Path

A network diagram is a graphical representation of a project's activities and their interdependencies. It provides a visual tool for project managers to plan, schedule, and analyze the flow of activities in a project. The network diagram is typically created using a technique called the Precedence Diagramming Method (PDM), which uses nodes and arrows to represent activities and their relationships.

In a network diagram, nodes represent activities, and arrows represent the dependencies between activities. There are four types of dependencies commonly used in network diagrams:

1. Finish-to-Start (FS): Activity B cannot start until Activity A finishes.
2. Start-to-Start (SS): Activity B cannot start until Activity A starts.
3. Finish-to-Finish (FF): Activity B cannot finish until Activity A finishes.
4. Start-to-Finish (SF): Activity B cannot finish until Activity A starts.

The critical path is the longest sequence of activities in a project that determines the minimum amount of time required to complete the project. It represents the activities that have zero slack or float, meaning any delay in these activities will directly impact the project's overall duration. The critical path is identified by calculating the total duration of each path in the network diagram and selecting the path with the longest duration.

Let's consider an example to understand network diagrams and critical paths:

Suppose we have a software development project with the following activities:

1. Requirements gathering (A)
2. Design (B)
3. Development (C)
4. Testing (D)
5. Deployment (E)

The dependencies between these activities are as follows:

A -> B (FS)
B -> C (FS)
C -> D (FS)
D -> E (FS)

To create a network diagram, we represent these activities as nodes and connect them with arrows according to their dependencies:

A --> B --> C --> D --> E

Each activity has an estimated duration, for example:

A: 5 days
B: 7 days

C: 10 days
D: 4 days
E: 6 days

To calculate the critical path, we determine the total duration of each path in the network diagram:

Path 1: A -> B -> C -> D -> E (5 + 7 + 10 + 4 + 6 = 32 days)

Since this path has the longest duration, it becomes the critical path for the project. Any delay in activities along this path will directly impact the overall project duration. Therefore, the project manager needs to closely monitor and manage these activities to ensure timely completion of the project.

7.4 Example

Problem:

You are managing a large construction project that involves building a high-rise building. The project has several complex tasks that need to be completed, and you want to determine the critical path for scheduling the project. The following information is available:

Task A: Foundation Preparation
- Duration: 10 days
- Predecessor(s): None

Task B: Structural Framework
- Duration: 15 days
- Predecessor(s): Task A

Task C: Electrical and Plumbing
- Duration: 12 days
- Predecessor(s): Task A

Task D: Exterior Finishing
- Duration: 20 days
- Predecessor(s): Task B

Task E: Interior Finishing
- Duration: 18 days
- Predecessor(s): Task B, Task C

Task F: Quality Control Inspections
- Duration: 5 days

- Predecessor(s): Task D, Task E

Task G: Final Clean-up and Handover
- Duration: 7 days
- Predecessor(s): Task F

Task H: Landscaping and Site Beautification
- Duration: 10 days
- Predecessor(s): Task G

Task I: Final Inspection and Sign-off
- Duration: 3 days
- Predecessor(s): Task H

Task J: Project Closure
- Duration: 2 days
- Predecessor(s): Task I

Solution:

To determine the critical path for the project scheduling, we need to find the longest path of dependent tasks that will determine the project's overall duration. This path is known as the critical path.

By analyzing the given information, we can construct a network diagram representing the project tasks and their dependencies:

To find the critical path, we calculate the earliest start and finish times for each task by following these steps:

1. Start with Task A: The earliest start time for Task A is day 0, and the earliest finish time is day 10.

2. Move to Task B: Since Task B depends on Task A, the earliest start time for Task B is the same as the earliest finish time of Task A (day 10). Therefore, the earliest finish time for Task B is day 25 (day 10 + 15).

3. Move to Task C: Similar to Task B, Task C depends on Task A. Hence, the earliest start time for Task C is day 10. The earliest finish time for Task C is day 22 (days 10 + 12).

4. Move to Task D: Task D depends on Task B, so its earliest start time is day 25. The earliest finish time for Task D is day 45 (day 25 + 20).

5. Move to Task E: Task E depends on both Task B and Task C. The earliest start time for Task E is the maximum of the earliest finish times of its predecessors, which is day 25 (Task B). Therefore, the earliest finish time for Task E is day 43 (day 25 + 18).

6. Move to Task F: Task F depends on both Task D and Task E. Its earliest start time is the maximum of the earliest finish times of its predecessors, which is day 45 (Task D). The earliest finish time for Task F is day 50 (day 45 + 5).

7. Move to Task G: Task G depends on Task F. Its earliest start time is day 50, and the earliest finish time for Task G is day 57 (day 50 + 7).

8. Move to Task H: Task H depends on Task G. Its earliest

start time is day 57, and the earliest finish time for Task H is day 67 (day 57 + 10).

9. Move to Task I: Task I depends on Task H. Its earliest start time is day 67, and the earliest finish time for Task I is day 70 (day 67 + 3).

10. Move to Task J: Task J depends on Task I. Its earliest start time is day 70, and the earliest finish time for Task J is day 72 (day 70 + 2).

The critical path is the longest path from the start (Task A) to the end (Task J) which consists of tasks with no slack time. In this case, the critical path is:

A -> B -> D -> F -> G -> H -> I -> J

Therefore, the critical path for this project scheduling is:

1. Task A (Foundation Preparation)
2. Task B (Structural Framework)
3. Task D (Exterior Finishing)
4. Task F (Quality Control Inspections)
5. Task G (Final Clean-up and Handover)
6. Task H (Landscaping and Site Beautification)
7. Task I (Final Inspection and Sign-off)
8. Task J (Project Closure)

The total duration of the critical path is 72 days. Any delay in tasks on the critical path will directly impact the overall project timeline.

7.5 Exercise

1. What is project scheduling?

2. Why is project scheduling important in project management?

3. What are the different types of project scheduling techniques?

4. What is a Gantt chart, and how is it used in project scheduling?

5. What is the critical path method (CPM) in project scheduling?

6. How is the critical path determined in a project network diagram?

7. What is the float or slack in project scheduling?

8. How can you calculate the earliest start time (ES) and earliest finish time (EF) in the CPM?

9. How can you calculate the latest start time (LS) and latest finish time (LF) in the CPM?

10. What is the difference between free float and total float in project scheduling?

11. How can you identify the critical path in a project network diagram?

12. What are the advantages of using the critical path method in project scheduling?

13. What are the limitations or challenges of using the critical path method?

14. How can you calculate the project duration using the critical path method?

15. How can you calculate the total float for an activity in the project network diagram?

16. How can you determine the activities with zero float in the project network diagram?

17. What is the impact of adding or removing activities on the critical path?

18. How can you compress the project schedule without changing the critical path?

19. What is resource leveling, and how does it affect project scheduling?

20. What is the difference between a milestone and a task in project scheduling?

21. How can you represent dependencies between activities in a project network diagram?

22. What is a finish-to-start dependency, and when is it used in project scheduling?

23. What is a start-to-start dependency, and when is it used in project scheduling?

24. What is a finish-to-finish dependency, and when is it used in project scheduling?

25. What is a start-to-finish dependency, and when is it used in project scheduling?

26. How can you calculate the total project float or total project slack?

27. What is the concept of crashing in project scheduling?

28. How does crashing an activity affect the project schedule and cost?

29. What is a milestone schedule, and when is it used in project management?

30. How can you identify the critical chain in a project schedule?

31. What is the concept of resource-constrained scheduling?

32. What is a resource histogram, and how is it used in project scheduling?

33. How can you calculate the project's early start, late start, early finish, and late finish times?

34. How can you determine the project's earliest and latest completion times?

35. What are some common scheduling challenges faced by project managers?

36. How can you handle schedule delays or changes in project scheduling?

37. What is the concept of lead time and lag time in project scheduling?

38. How can you calculate the expected duration of a project using three-point estimating?

39. How does the critical path method help in identifying potential risks in a project?

40. How can you calculate the critical path for a project with multiple paths?

41. You are managing a construction project with multiple interconnected tasks. Each task has a defined duration, and there are dependencies between the tasks. Your goal is to determine the critical path and calculate the total duration of the project.

Task List:
Task A: Duration = 5 days
Task B: Duration = 3 days
Task C: Duration = 7 days
Task D: Duration = 4 days
Task E: Duration = 6 days

Dependencies:
Task A must be completed before Task B can start.
Task A must be completed before Task C can start.
Task B must be completed before Task D can start.
Task C must be completed before Task E can start.
Task D must be completed before Task E can start.
Calculate the critical path duration and identify the tasks involved in the critical path.

42. You are managing a software development project with multiple tasks. Each task has a defined duration, and there are dependencies between the tasks. Your goal is to determine the slack time for each task, which represents the amount of time a task can be delayed without affecting the project's overall duration.

Task List:
Task A: Duration = 6 days
Task B: Duration = 4 days
Task C: Duration = 5 days
Task D: Duration = 3 days
Task E: Duration = 7 days

Dependencies:
Task A must be completed before Task C can start.
Task A must be completed before Task D can start.
Task B must be completed before Task E can start.
Task C must be completed before Task E can start.
Task D must be completed before Task E can start.

Calculate the slack time for each task and identify the tasks with zero slack time, indicating they are on the critical path.

8 Resource, Budget, Procurement, Quality, Communication, and Risk Management Planning

8.1 Resource Planning

Resource planning is the process of identifying, allocating, and managing resources to accomplish specific tasks or projects efficiently. It involves estimating resource requirements, determining the availability of resources, and optimizing their utilization. Effective resource planning helps organizations meet project deadlines, control costs, and achieve their objectives. Mathematical examples can be used to illustrate various aspects of resource planning, such as resource allocation and optimization.

1. Resource Allocation:
Resource allocation involves assigning available resources to different activities or tasks in a project. It ensures that resources are utilized effectively and efficiently. Let's consider a simple example:

Example 1:
A construction company has three ongoing projects: Project A, Project B, and Project C. They have a team of 10 workers available for these projects. The company needs to allocate the workers optimally based on the estimated work hours required for each project. The estimated work hours for each project are as follows:

- Project A: 100 hours
- Project B: 80 hours
- Project C: 120 hours

To allocate the workers optimally, we can use proportional

allocation based on the estimated work hours. In this case, we can calculate the proportion of workers allocated to each project by dividing the estimated work hours by the total estimated work hours:

- Project A: (100 / (100 + 80 + 120)) * 10 workers = 3.33 workers
- Project B: (80 / (100 + 80 + 120)) * 10 workers = 2.67 workers
- Project C: (120 / (100 + 80 + 120)) * 10 workers = 4 workers

Since the number of workers must be whole numbers, we can round the calculated values:

- Project A: 3 workers
- Project B: 3 workers
- Project C: 4 workers

By allocating resources in this manner, the construction company ensures that the available workers are distributed proportionally based on the estimated work hours for each project.

2. Resource Optimization:
Resource optimization aims to maximize resource utilization while minimizing costs or time. It involves finding the best allocation of resources that achieves the desired outcomes efficiently. Let's consider an optimization problem:

Example 2:
A manufacturing company produces two types of products: Product X and Product Y. The company has a limited number of machines available for production and wants to maximize the total production volume of both products.

The production time required for each product on each machine and the machine availability is given in the table below:

	Machine 1	Machine 2	Machine 3
Product X	2 hours	1 hour	3 hours
Product Y	4 hours	2 hours	1 hour
Availability	100 hours	50 hours	80 hours

Let's define the decision variables as follows:
- X: The number of units of Product X to produce
- Y: The number of units of Product Y to produce

The objective is to maximize the total production volume (X + Y) while considering the constraints of machine availability. The objective function and constraints can be formulated as follows:

Objective function: Maximize X + Y
Constraints:
1. $2X + 4Y <= 100$ (Machine 1 availability)
2. $X + 2Y <= 50$ (Machine 2 availability)
3. $3X + Y <= 80$ (Machine 3 availability)
4. $X, Y >= 0$ (Non-negativity constraint)

By solving this linear programming problem using techniques such as the simplex method or graphical method, we can determine the optimal values for X and Y, which would maximize the total production volume given the machine availability.

These examples demonstrate the application of mathematical techniques in resource planning. Resource allocation ensures the optimal distribution of resources across tasks or projects, while resource optimization focuses on maximizing resource utilization while considering constraints and objectives. By employing mathematical models, organizations can make informed decisions and effectively plan their resources to achieve desired outcomes.

8.2 Budget Planning

Budget planning is a crucial aspect of project management that involves estimating and allocating resources to ensure the successful execution of a project within the available financial constraints. It requires careful consideration of various factors, including project scope, timeline, resource requirements, and cost estimates. In this note, we will explore the key steps involved in budget planning and provide mathematical examples to illustrate the concepts.

1. Define the Project Scope: Clearly defining the project scope is essential as it determines the boundaries of the project and the activities to be included. A well-defined scope helps in accurately estimating the budget. For example, consider a software development project to create a new mobile application.

2. Identify Activities and Resources: Break down the project into smaller tasks or activities. Identify the resources required for each activity, such as personnel, equipment, materials, and external services. For instance, in our mobile application project, activities might include requirements gathering, design, coding, testing, and deployment. The resources needed may include developers, designers, testers, and servers.

3. Estimate Activity Durations: Determine the time required to complete each activity. Accurate duration estimation helps in determining the labor costs associated with the project. For example, if the coding activity is estimated to

202

take 200 hours and the hourly rate for a developer is $50, then the labor cost for coding would be 200 hours * $50/hour = $10,000.

4. Determine Resource Costs: Calculate the costs associated with each resource required for the project. This may include salaries, benefits, equipment maintenance, and any other applicable costs. For instance, if a designer's monthly salary is $5,000, and the project duration is three months, the designer's cost would be $5,000 * 3 = $15,000.

5. Quantify Material and Equipment Costs: Identify the materials and equipment needed for the project and estimate their costs. This may include hardware, software licenses, office supplies, or any other tangible items required. For example, if the mobile application project requires a specific software license costing $500, that cost would be included in the budget.

6. Calculate Direct Costs: Sum up the costs directly attributed to the project activities, including labor costs, resource costs, and material/equipment costs. For instance, the total direct cost for the mobile application project would be the sum of labor costs, resource costs, and material/equipment costs.

7. Consider Indirect Costs: Indirect costs are expenses not directly tied to specific project activities but necessary for overall project management, such as administrative overhead, utilities, or rent. Estimate and allocate these costs based on an appropriate allocation method, such as a percentage of direct costs or specific expense items. For

example, if the indirect costs are estimated to be 20% of the total direct costs, then the indirect cost for the mobile application project would be 20% * (total direct costs).

8. Incorporate Contingency: It is wise to include a contingency amount in the budget to account for unforeseen events or risks that may arise during the project. The contingency is usually expressed as a percentage of the total budget. For example, if a 10% contingency is included, then the contingency amount would be 10% * (total direct costs + indirect costs).

9. Calculate the Total Project Budget: Sum up the direct costs, indirect costs, and contingency to arrive at the total project budget. The total budget represents the estimated cost required to complete the project. For instance, if the direct costs are $100,000, indirect costs are $20,000, and contingency is $12,000, then the total project budget would be $100,000 + $20,000 + $12,000 = $132,000.

It is important to note that budget planning is an iterative

process. As the project progresses and more information becomes available, the budget may need to be revised and adjusted accordingly.

Mathematical Example:
Let's consider a construction project to build a residential complex. The project has the following key details:

- Project duration: 12 months
- Labor costs: $50 per hour for construction workers

- Number of workers: 10
- Average working hours per day: 8 hours
- Number of working days in a month: 22 days
- Material costs: $100,000
- Equipment costs: $50,000
- Indirect costs: 15% of direct costs

To calculate the budget for this project, we will go through the steps mentioned above:

1. Define the Project Scope: Residential complex construction project.

2. Identify Activities and Resources: Activities include site preparation, foundation construction, structural work, electrical work, plumbing work, interior finishing, and landscaping. Resources include construction workers, supervisors, construction equipment, and materials.

3. Estimate Activity Durations: Assume each activity takes one month to complete.

4. Determine Resource Costs: Construction workers are paid $50 per hour, and they work 8 hours per day. In a month, with 22 working days, the labor cost per worker would be $50 * 8 * 22 = $8,800. Considering 10 workers, the total labor cost would be $8,800 * 10 = $88,000.

5. Quantify Material and Equipment Costs: Material costs are estimated at $100,000, and equipment costs are $50,000.

6. Calculate Direct Costs: The direct cost would be the sum

of labor costs, material costs, and equipment costs: $88,000 (labor) + $100,000 (material) + $50,000 (equipment) = $238,000.

7. Consider Indirect Costs: Indirect costs are estimated to be 15% of the direct costs. Therefore, the indirect costs would be 15% * $238,000 = $35,700.

8. Incorporate Contingency: Assume a 10% contingency, so the contingency amount would be 10% * ($238,000 + $35,700) = $27,870.

9. Calculate the Total Project Budget: The total project budget would be the sum of direct costs, indirect costs, and contingency: $238,000 (direct costs) + $35,700 (indirect costs) + $27,870 (contingency) = $301,570.

In this example, the total budget for the residential complex construction project would be $301,570. This budget represents the estimated cost required to complete the project within the specified scope and timeline, considering the labor, materials, equipment, and other associated costs.

8.3 Procurement Planning

Procurement planning is an essential component of project management that involves identifying, acquiring, and managing the necessary goods, services, and resources to successfully execute a project. It includes various activities such as determining procurement requirements, selecting appropriate suppliers, establishing contracts, and monitoring procurement processes. In this note, we will explore the key aspects of procurement planning and provide multiple mathematical examples to illustrate some common procurement calculations.

1. Determining Procurement Requirements:
   - Quantity Calculation: To determine the number of goods or services required, you can use mathematical formulas or historical data. For example, if a construction project requires cement, you can calculate the estimated quantity based on the volume of concrete needed and the ratio of cement to concrete.

   Example 1: A construction project needs to pour 500 cubic meters of concrete. The cement-to-concrete ratio is 1:4. What is the estimated quantity of cement required?

   Solution:
   Cement quantity = (Concrete volume) x (Cement-to-concrete ratio)
   Cement quantity = 500 cubic meters x $1/4$
   Cement quantity = 125 cubic meters

   - Timeframe Calculation: When planning procurement, it

is important to consider lead times and delivery schedules. You can use mathematical calculations to determine the required ordering and delivery dates. For example, if a project requires equipment that has a lead time of 30 days, you can calculate the ordering date by subtracting the lead time from the project start date.

Example 2: A project is scheduled to start on June 1st, and equipment with a lead time of 30 days is required. What is the ordering date for the equipment?

Solution:
Ordering date = Project start date - Lead time
Ordering date = June 1st - 30 days
Ordering date = May 2nd

2. Selecting Suppliers:
- Price Comparison: Mathematical calculations can be used to compare prices from different suppliers and select the most cost-effective option. For example, if you receive quotes from two suppliers for a specific item, you can calculate the price per unit to determine which supplier offers the best deal.

Example 3: Supplier A offers 500 units of a product for $1,500, and Supplier B offers 600 units of the same product for $1,800. Which supplier provides a better price per unit?

Solution:
Price per unit for Supplier A = Total cost / Number of units
Price per unit for Supplier A = $1,500 / 500 units

Price per unit for Supplier A = $3 per unit

Price per unit for Supplier B = Total cost / Number of units
Price per unit for Supplier B = $1,800 / 600 units
Price per unit for Supplier B = $3 per unit

Both suppliers offer the same price per unit, so the decision can be based on other factors such as reputation, quality, or additional services.

3. Establishing Contracts:
   - Total Cost Calculation: When establishing contracts, it is crucial to calculate the total cost, including any additional charges or discounts. Mathematical calculations can help determine the overall expenses.

Example 4: A service contract includes a monthly fee of $1,000 for 12 months. The supplier offers a 5% discount if the contract is paid in full upfront. What is the total cost with and without the discount?

Solution:
Total cost without discount = Monthly fee x Number of months
Total cost without discount = $1,000 x 12 months
Total cost without discount = $12,000

Total cost with discount = Total cost without discount - Discount amount
Discount amount = Total cost without discount x Discount rate

Discount amount = $12,000 x 5%
Discount amount = $600

Total cost with discount = $12,000 - $600
Total cost with discount = $11,400

4. Monitoring Procurement Processes:
- Cost Performance Calculation: To monitor the cost performance of procurement activities, you can calculate metrics such as cost variance (CV) and cost performance index (CPI). These indicators help assess whether the procurement processes are within budget and on track.

Example 5: The budgeted cost of a procurement item is $10,000, but the actual cost is $12,000. Calculate the cost variance (CV) and cost performance index (CPI).

Solution:
Cost Variance (CV) = Budgeted Cost - Actual Cost
CV = $10,000 - $12,000
CV = -$2,000 (negative value indicates cost overrun)

Cost Performance Index (CPI) = Earned Value (EV) / Actual Cost (AC)
CPI = $10,000 / $12,000
CPI = 0.83 (a value less than 1 indicates cost overrun)

These examples provide a glimpse into the mathematical calculations involved in procurement planning for project management. However, it's important to note that procurement planning encompasses many other aspects, such as risk assessment, quality assurance, and stakeholder management. Effective procurement planning requires a comprehensive approach that combines mathematical analysis with qualitative considerations to ensure successful project execution.

8.4 Quality Planning

Quality planning is a crucial aspect of project management that focuses on defining the quality standards and objectives for a project and outlining the strategies and processes to achieve those standards. It involves a systematic approach to identifying, assessing, and mitigating risks that can impact the quality of project deliverables. By implementing effective quality planning, project managers can ensure that the project meets or exceeds the expectations of stakeholders.

Here are some key steps and mathematical examples related to quality planning in project management:

1. Defining Quality Objectives:
   Quality objectives are the measurable goals that define the desired level of quality for project deliverables. These objectives should be specific, measurable, attainable, relevant, and time-bound (SMART). For example, consider a software development project where the quality objective is to have fewer than 5 bugs per 1,000 lines of code.

2. Identifying Quality Standards:
   Quality standards are the established criteria against which the project deliverables will be evaluated. They define the minimum acceptable level of quality for the project. These standards can be based on industry best practices, customer requirements, or regulatory guidelines. For example, in a construction project, the quality standard for concrete strength might be defined as a compressive strength of at

least 30 megapascals (MPa) after 28 days.

3. Quality Assurance:

Quality assurance involves the processes and activities carried out during the project execution phase to ensure that the project is being implemented according to the defined quality standards. It includes activities such as inspections, audits, and reviews to identify and rectify any deviations from the quality objectives. For instance, in a manufacturing project, regular quality inspections might be conducted to check the dimensions of the produced components against the specified tolerances.

4. Quality Control:

Quality control focuses on monitoring and verifying the project deliverables to ensure they meet the defined quality standards. Statistical techniques and control charts are often used to analyze and track the quality of data collected during the project. For example, in a call center project, the average call handling time can be monitored using control charts to ensure it remains within the acceptable range.

5. Risk Management:

Risk management plays a vital role in quality planning by identifying potential risks that may impact the project's quality objectives. Quantitative risk analysis techniques, such as probability and impact assessment, can be employed to prioritize and quantify these risks. For example, in a construction project, the risk of material shortages can be assessed by calculating the probability of delays caused by supplier issues and estimating the impact on the project schedule.

6. Continuous Improvement:

Continuous improvement is an integral part of quality planning. It involves evaluating project performance, analyzing lessons learned, and implementing corrective actions to enhance the project's quality. Statistical process control (SPC) techniques, such as Pareto analysis or cause-and-effect diagrams, can be used to identify the root causes of quality issues and develop appropriate corrective measures. For instance, in a software development project, the defect data collected during testing can be analyzed using Pareto analysis to identify the most frequent types of defects and prioritize improvement efforts accordingly.

Mathematical Examples:

Example 1:

Suppose a project aims to achieve a defect rate of less than 2% for a manufactured product. During quality control inspections, a sample of 500 units is taken, and it is found that 7 units have defects. To assess if the defect rate meets the objective, we can use the formula for defect rate:

Defect rate = (Defective units / Total units) * 100
Defect rate = (7 / 500) * 100
Defect rate = 1.4%

In this example, the defect rate is lower than the objective of 2%, indicating that the quality standard is being met.

Example 2:
Consider a project where the goal is to

 reduce customer complaints by at least 20% compared to the previous year. In the previous year, there were 500 customer complaints. To calculate the target number of complaints for the current year, we can use the formula:

Target complaints = Previous complaints - (Previous complaints * Reduction percentage)
Target complaints = 500 - (500 * 0.20)
Target complaints = 400

In this case, the target number of complaints for the current year is 400, reflecting a 20% reduction from the previous year.

These mathematical examples demonstrate how quantitative analysis can be applied within quality planning to set quantifiable objectives, monitor progress, and evaluate project performance.

8.5 Communication Planning

Communication planning is a crucial aspect of project management that involves developing a systematic approach to ensure effective and efficient communication among project stakeholders. A well-executed communication plan facilitates the smooth flow of information, fosters collaboration, manages expectations, and helps in achieving project objectives. In this note, we will discuss the key elements of communication planning and provide multiple mathematical examples to illustrate their application.

1. Identify Stakeholders:

The first step in communication planning is to identify all the project stakeholders. Stakeholders can include project sponsors, team members, clients, vendors, and other individuals or groups impacted by the project. Creating a stakeholder register helps to establish a clear understanding of who needs to be communicated with and what their communication needs are.

Example: Consider a construction project where the stakeholders include the project manager, architects, contractors, subcontractors, suppliers, and local authorities. Each stakeholder has specific information requirements and expectations that must be addressed in the communication plan.

2. Determine Communication Objectives:

Next, it is essential to define the communication objectives for the project. These objectives outline the desired outcomes of communication activities, such as informing stakeholders, seeking their input, gaining their commitment, or resolving conflicts. Clear objectives help project managers tailor their communication strategies to achieve specific goals.

Example: In a software development project, the communication objectives may include sharing progress updates with the client, gathering feedback from end-users, and providing status reports to project sponsors. Each objective requires different communication methods and frequencies.

3. Define Communication Channels:

Once the stakeholders and communication objectives are identified, project managers must select appropriate communication channels to deliver information effectively. Communication channels can be classified into two types: formal and informal. Formal channels include written reports, emails, meetings, presentations, and project management software. Informal channels involve casual conversations, social media, and impromptu discussions.

Example: For a marketing campaign project, formal communication channels could include weekly status reports, progress meetings, and presentations to the management team. Informal channels may include instant messaging tools or informal discussions during team lunches.

4. Determine Communication Frequency and Timing:
Timing plays a vital role in communication planning. Project managers must determine the frequency of communication with different stakeholders and establish deadlines for delivering information. The communication plan should include a schedule indicating when and how often various types of communication will occur.

Example: In an event management project, regular communication may be required with vendors to confirm delivery schedules, manage inventory, and address any issues. The communication frequency with vendors may be daily or weekly, depending on the stage of the project.

5. Establish Communication Protocols:
To ensure consistency and clarity in project communication, it is crucial to establish communication protocols. These protocols define the guidelines for communication, including the format, language, tone, and level of detail. They help maintain professionalism and minimize misunderstandings.

Example: In a research project, the communication

protocol might specify that all written reports should follow a specific template, include relevant data analysis, and be written in a clear, concise manner. This protocol ensures that all project stakeholders receive consistent and meaningful information.

6. Monitor and Adjust the Communication Plan:
Finally, project managers need to continuously monitor the effectiveness of the communication plan and make adjustments as needed. Regular feedback from stakeholders, progress evaluations, and lessons learned can help identify areas for improvement and ensure that communication remains aligned with project goals.

Example: In a manufacturing project, the project manager might conduct periodic surveys to gather feedback from the production team regarding the effectiveness of communication channels and the clarity of instructions. Based on the feedback, adjustments can be made to the communication plan to address any gaps or issues.

In summary, communication planning is a vital component of project management that contains identifying stakeholders, setting communication objectives, selecting appropriate channels, determining frequency and timing, establishing protocols, and monitoring effectiveness. By following a systematic communication plan, project managers can enhance collaboration, manage expectations, and increase the likelihood of project success.

Please note that the mathematical examples provided here are intended to illustrate the concepts of communication planning in a project management context. The examples do not involve complex mathematical calculations but rather focus on understanding the application of communication planning principles.

8.6 Risk Management Planning

Risk management planning is a critical component of project management that involves identifying, analyzing, and mitigating potential risks that may impact the success of a project. It helps project managers proactively address uncertainties and develop strategies to minimize or eliminate the negative effects of risks. In this note, I will explain the key steps involved in risk management planning and provide some mathematical examples to illustrate the concepts.

1. Risk Identification:
The first step in risk management planning is to identify all potential risks that may arise during the project lifecycle. Risks can be categorized into various types, such as technical risks, external risks, organizational risks, and so on. The project team should brainstorm and use techniques like SWOT analysis, interviews, checklists, and historical data to identify as many risks as possible.

Example 1: Consider a construction project. One potential risk could be adverse weather conditions, which may cause delays in the project schedule. Another risk could be a shortage of skilled labor, leading to difficulties in completing the project on time.

2. Risk Analysis:

Once risks are identified, the next step is to analyze and evaluate their potential impact and likelihood of occurrence. This analysis helps prioritize risks based on their significance and allows project managers to focus on high-impact risks. Two key parameters used in risk analysis are the probability of occurrence (PO) and the impact severity (IS).

Example 2: Suppose a software development project has identified a risk related to a possible security breach. The project team estimates that there is a 30% probability (PO) of a security breach occurring, and if it does happen, the impact severity (IS) will be high, potentially leading to data loss and reputational damage.

3. Risk Assessment:

Risk assessment involves combining the probability of occurrence and impact severity to calculate the overall risk rating of each identified risk. This rating helps in prioritizing risks and deciding on appropriate mitigation strategies. Various mathematical models, such as Risk Priority Number (RPN), can be used to calculate the risk rating.

Example 3: Consider a manufacturing project that has identified a risk related to the unavailability of raw materials. The project team assigns a probability of occurrence (PO) of 20% and an impact severity (IS) of the medium. The risk rating can be calculated as RPN = PO x IS, which in this case would be 20% x Medium = 0.2 x 3 = 0.6.

4. Risk Response Planning:

Based on the risk assessment, project managers need to develop appropriate risk response plans to address each identified risk. There are four common risk response strategies: avoid, transfer, mitigate, and accept. The selection of the response strategy depends on the risk rating and the organization's risk appetite.

Example 4: For a marketing project, a risk related to a competitor launching a similar product could be identified. The project team decides to implement a risk response strategy of "mitigate" by investing in market research and product differentiation to minimize the impact of competition.

5. Risk Monitoring and Control:

Once the risk response plans are implemented, it is essential to continuously monitor and control risks throughout the project. This involves tracking the effectiveness of risk mitigation measures, identifying new risks that may arise, and adjusting the risk management plan accordingly. Regular risk reviews and updates are necessary to ensure that risks are properly managed throughout the project lifecycle.

Example 5: In a research project, a risk related to data integrity is identified. The project team implements measures such as regular backups, data validation checks, and access controls to mitigate the risk. Throughout the project, regular monitoring and audits are conducted to ensure the effectiveness of these measures.

In summary, risk management planning is a systematic approach to identifying, analyzing, and mitigating potential risks in project management. By following these steps and utilizing mathematical models, project managers can proactively address uncertainties and improve the chances of project success.

8.7 Exercise

Resource Planning:

1. What are the key resources required for the project?

2. How will you determine the resource requirements for each project task?

3. What factors will you consider when assigning resources to specific tasks?

4. How will you handle resource conflicts or bottlenecks during the project?

5. What contingency plans do you have in place for unexpected changes in resource availability?

6. How will you ensure that resources are effectively utilized throughout the project?

7. How will you track and monitor resource usage and availability?

8. What steps will you take to address any resource shortages or overages?

Budget Planning:

9. How will you estimate the project budget?

10. What cost categories will be included in the project budget?

11. What techniques will you use to control project costs?

12. How will you handle cost variances and deviations from the budget?

13. What measures will you take to ensure that the project stays within budget?

14. How will you track and monitor project expenses?

15. What approvals or authorizations are required for budget adjustments?

16. How will you handle unexpected cost increases or changes in project scope?

Procurement Planning:

17. What items or services will need to be procured for the project?

18. How will you determine the procurement method for each item or service?

19. What criteria will you use to evaluate potential suppliers or vendors?

20. How will you ensure that procurement activities are aligned with project timelines?

21. What contractual terms and conditions will be included in procurement agreements?

22. How will you manage and monitor supplier performance?

23. What steps will you take to resolve any issues or disputes with suppliers?

24. How will you handle changes or modifications to procurement requirements?

Quality Planning:

25. How will you define and measure quality for the project?

26. What quality standards or benchmarks will be used?

27. What quality control activities will be conducted

throughout the project?

28. How will you ensure that quality requirements are communicated to all stakeholders?

29. What processes or procedures will be put in place to prevent or address quality issues?

30. How will you document and track quality-related metrics and indicators?

31. What measures will you take to continuously improve quality during the project?

32. How will you conduct quality audits or inspections?

Communication Planning:

33. Who are the key stakeholders for the project?

34. What communication channels and tools will be used to reach stakeholders?

35. How will you determine the frequency and format of project communications?

36. What information will be included in project status reports?

37. How will you handle communication with remote or geographically dispersed teams?

38. How will you address and resolve communication barriers or conflicts?

39. How will you ensure that all stakeholders are kept informed and engaged?

40. How will you collect and incorporate feedback from stakeholders?

41. What contingency plans do you have in place for communication disruptions?

42. How will you manage and prioritize project risks?

43. What strategies will you employ to mitigate identified risks?

44. How will you monitor and track risk exposure and likelihood?

45. How will you handle risk events or incidents if they occur?

46. How will you communicate risk-related information to stakeholders?

47. How will you ensure that risk management activities are integrated into the project plan?

48. What processes or procedures will be followed for risk identification and assessment?

49. How will you update the risk management plan as the project progresses?

50. How will you ensure that risk responses are implemented effectively?

Risk Management Planning

51. What are the key steps involved in developing a comprehensive risk management plan for a project or organization?

52. How do you identify and prioritize potential risks during the risk management planning process?

53. What are some common strategies and techniques for mitigating or minimizing identified risks in a risk management plan?

54. How do you monitor and evaluate the effectiveness of risk management strategies implemented in a project or organization?

55. What role does communication play in risk management planning, and how can effective communication contribute to the success of risk management effort

9 Project Implementation and Completion

9.1 Implementing and Completing

Project implementation and completion are crucial phases in any project lifecycle. These stages involve executing the planned activities, monitoring progress, addressing issues, and successfully delivering the desired outcomes. Mathematical examples can help illustrate various aspects of project implementation and completion, including planning, scheduling, resource allocation, and evaluation. In this note, we will explore these concepts in detail, accompanied by multiple mathematical examples.
'

1. Planning and Scheduling:
Before starting a project, careful planning and scheduling are necessary to ensure a systematic approach to implementation. This involves determining the project scope, defining deliverables, identifying tasks, estimating durations, and sequencing activities.
Example 1: Let's consider a construction project to build a house. The project scope includes tasks such as excavation, foundation, framing, plumbing, electrical work, interior finishing, and landscaping. Each task has an estimated duration, as shown below:

Task	Duration (in weeks)
Excavation	2
Foundation	3
Framing	4
Plumbing	2
Electrical work	3
Interior finishing	4
Landscaping	2

By sequencing these tasks based on their dependencies, we can create a project schedule. For example, the foundation task cannot start until the excavation is complete. The schedule may look like this:

Week	Task
1-2	Excavation
3-5	Foundation
6-9	Framing
10-11	Plumbing
12-14	Electrical work
15-18	Interior finishing
19-20	Landscaping

2. Resource Allocation:

During project implementation, resources need to be allocated efficiently to ensure timely completion. Resources include manpower, materials, equipment, and finances. Proper allocation and optimization of resources are essential to avoid delays and cost overruns.

Example 2: Let's continue with the construction project example. The project requires three skilled workers and one crane. The availability of these resources is as follows:

Resource	Availability (in weeks)
Skilled workers	12
Crane	6

To allocate resources efficiently, we can create a resource schedule by assigning resources to specific tasks based on their availability and requirements. For example:

Week	Task	Resources
1-2	Excavation	3 workers
3-5	Foundation	3 workers
3-5	Foundation	1 crane
6-9	Framing	3 workers
10-11	Plumbing	3 workers
12-14	Electrical work	3 workers
12-14	Electrical work	1 crane
15-18	Interior finishing	3 workers
19-20	Landscaping	3 workers

By optimizing resource allocation, we ensure that the required resources are available when needed, minimizing idle time and maximizing productivity.

3. Monitoring and Control:
During project implementation, regular monitoring and control are necessary to track progress, identify deviations, and take corrective actions. Key performance indicators (KPIs) are used to measure project performance and compare it against the planned targets.

Example 3: Let's consider a software development project. One of the KPIs is the number of lines of code (LOC) written per week. The planned target is 500 LOC per week. The actual number of LOC written in the first five weeks is as follows:

Week	Actual LOC
1	480
2	520
3	510
4	490
5	520

To monitor project progress, we can calculate the variance between actual and planned values. For example:

Week	Actual LOC	Planned LOC	Variance
1	480	500	-20
2	520	500	+20
3	510	500	+10
4	490	500	-10
5	520	500	+20

Positive variances indicate progress exceeding the plan, while negative variances signify a lag in progress. Monitoring such KPIs helps project managers identify potential bottlenecks and take corrective actions to bring the project back on track.

4. Evaluation and Completion:
Once all project activities are completed, it is essential to evaluate the project's success against the defined objectives and criteria. This evaluation allows stakeholders to assess the project's performance, identify lessons learned, and determine areas for improvement in future projects.

Example 4: Let's consider an advertising campaign project to increase brand awareness. The success criteria include measuring the number of social media impressions, website visits, and customer inquiries. The actual results achieved are as follows:

Metric	Actual Value
Social media	2,500,000 impressions
Website visits	100,000
Customer inquiries	5,000

By comparing the actual results against the defined success criteria, stakeholders can evaluate the project's success. In this case, if the success criteria were to achieve at least 2 million social media impressions, 80,000 website visits, and 4,000 customer inquiries, the project can be deemed successful.

Project implementation and completion involve careful planning, scheduling, resource allocation, monitoring, and evaluation. Mathematical examples, as demonstrated above, can help in understanding and illustrating these concepts.

By effectively applying mathematical techniques and analysis, project managers can ensure successful project outcomes within defined timelines, budgets, and quality parameters.

9.2 Celebration

Dear Team,

I am delighted to inform you that we have completed our recent project, and I want to express my heartfelt appreciation for your outstanding efforts, dedication, and hard work. Your commitment and collaboration have been instrumental in achieving this significant milestone, and I believe it calls for a grand celebration.

To acknowledge and celebrate our collective success, I propose organizing a memorable event that not only recognizes our accomplishments but also fosters team spirit and camaraderie. A well-deserved celebration will not only provide a sense of closure but also serve as an opportunity for us to relax, reflect on our achievements, and recharge for future endeavors.

Here are a few ideas for our celebration:

1. Team Outing: Plan a day trip to a nearby amusement park, beach, or recreational center where everyone can participate in various activities such as team-building exercises, sports, and games. This will encourage team bonding and create an enjoyable atmosphere for everyone.

2. Dinner and Awards Night: Arrange a formal dinner at a local restaurant or banquet hall, where we can dress up, socialize, and recognize outstanding performances. Prepare personalized certificates or trophies for team members who have excelled in their roles or gone above and beyond to

ensure the project's success.

3. Team Building Activities: Engage in team-building exercises that promote collaboration and communication. Activities like escape rooms, paintball, or outdoor adventure challenges can help strengthen the bonds among team members and enhance problem-solving skills.

4. Themed Party: Organize a themed party at the office or an external venue. Encourage team members to dress up according to the chosen theme and arrange activities like games, music, and dance to create a festive atmosphere.

5. Volunteer or Philanthropic Activities: Consider participating in a volunteer or philanthropic event as a team. This could involve organizing a charity drive, visiting a local community center, or supporting a cause that aligns with our team's values. Giving back to the community will not only provide a sense of fulfillment but also strengthen the team's unity.

6. Team Trip or Retreat: Plan a weekend getaway or team retreat at a serene location away from the office. This will allow everyone to relax, unwind, and engage in team-building activities while enjoying the scenic surroundings.

Remember, the goal of the celebration is not just to have fun, but also to acknowledge the collective achievements, appreciate individual contributions, and reinforce the bonds within our team. The specific celebration format can be tailored to our team's preferences and budget, but the underlying intention should be to recognize and honor the hard work and dedication exhibited by each team member.

I encourage everyone to share their ideas and preferences for the celebration. Let's come together to make this event a memorable one and show our appreciation for the exceptional work we have accomplished.

Once again, thank you all for your unwavering commitment and exceptional performance. Your contributions have been invaluable, and I look forward to celebrating our success together.

Best regards,

Dr. Prasun Bhattacharjee.

9.3 Exercise

1. What is the timeline for the project implementation and completion?

2. What are the key milestones and deliverables for the project?

3. What resources, both human and material, are required for the project implementation?

4. How will the project be divided into phases or stages?

5. What is the estimated budget for the project, and how will it be allocated?

6. What are the potential risks and challenges that could affect project implementation and completion?

7. Are there any legal or regulatory requirements that need to be considered during the project implementation?

8. What are the success criteria or key performance indicators (KPIs) for measuring the project's completion?

9. How will project progress be monitored and reported?

10. What communication channels and tools will be used to facilitate collaboration among project team members?

11. Are there any dependencies or interdependencies with other projects or stakeholders that need to be managed?

12. How will changes or scope adjustments be handled during project implementation?

13. What contingency plans are in place to address unexpected issues or delays?

14. What quality assurance measures will be implemented to ensure project deliverables meet the required standards?

15. What training or knowledge transfer activities are planned to support project implementation and completion?

16. How will the project be transitioned to the operations or maintenance phase after completion?

17. What documentation and artifacts will be produced as part of the project implementation and completion?

18. How will project outcomes be evaluated to determine if the objectives were met?

19. What lessons learned from previous projects will be applied to enhance project implementation and completion?

20. How will stakeholder satisfaction and feedback be gathered and incorporated into the project implementation process?

ABOUT THE AUTHOR

Dr. Prasun Bhattacharjee is a Ph.D. in Engineering (Awarded by the Department of Mechanical Engineering of the prestigious Jadavpur University of Kolkata, India). His numerous scientific contributions have been published in distinguished peer-reviewed journals. Prasun has also presented his research works at several international conferences held in the USA and European nations. He is currently a member of the Indian Institute of Welding and the Association for Information Systems. His research mainly focuses on employing artificial intelligence techniques for enhancing the performance of wind power generation systems. Dr. Bhattacharjee earned the university medal of the Maulana Abul Kalam Azad University of Technology, West Bengal while studying for the Master of Technology degree in Industrial Engineering and Management. He has also worked for the distinguished TATA group as a Systems Engineer after passing out from the Kalyani Government Engineering College as a mechanical engineer. Dr. Bhattacharjee has traveled extensively to almost every corner of India and 23 foreign nations with his parents. He loves to share his travel experiences with other fellow nomads for helping them witness the wonders of the world on their own. You can enjoy his exhilarating travel videos on his YouTube channel (https://www.youtube.com/c/prasunbhattacharjee1206) or visit the author on Twitter (@Prasun6official). Dr. Bhattacharjee is presently serving as a lecturer in Mechanical Engineering.